"Sam Storms has written a wo
live in the power of God's forg
Jack Deere, Associate Pro
Theological Seminary; author, *Surprised by the Power of the Spirit*

"For Christians who are being sanctified, wrestling with sin is an ongoing, never-ending struggle. This book beautifully underlines, makes bold, and highlights what God tells us he'll do with our sins. If you're struggling with a secret sin, battling a recurring sin, or continually regretting a past sin, this book will ease your soul and lift your head."
Sarah Eekhoff Zylstra, Senior Writer and Faith-and-Work Editor, The Gospel Coalition

"Sin and salvation are inextricably linked. Failing to understand or believe what Christ has done with our sins can cause us to question the validity of our salvation. That is not what God intended. Read this stellar book by Sam Storms to rediscover what it means to be cleansed. Start to dance with joy when you remember God trampled your sins underfoot, and draw near to him as you embrace the profound truth that he remembers your sins no more. Settle the issue of sin in your life, learn what God has done for you, and start rejoicing in your salvation! Storms will teach you how."
Janet Parshall, Host and Executive Producer, *In the Market with Janet Parshall*

"This book, written with pastoral humility and prophetic insight, brims with gospel hope. Christ has defeated our sin once and for all—we now fight from acceptance, not toward it; from victory, not in hope of it. Every book I read by Storms both challenges and encourages me, and this one is no exception."
J. D. Greear, Pastor, The Summit Church, Raleigh-Durham, North Carolina; author, *Just Ask!*

A Dozen Things God Did with Your Sin

Other Crossway Books by Sam Storms

Chosen for Life: The Case for Divine Election, 2007

The Hope of Glory: 100 Daily Meditations on Colossians, 2008

Kept for Jesus: What the New Testament Really Teaches about Assurance of Salvation and Eternal Security, 2015

More Precious Than Gold: 50 Daily Meditations on the Psalms, 2009

Packer on the Christian Life: Knowing God in Christ, Walking by the Spirit, 2015

Signs of the Spirit: An Interpretation of Jonathan Edwards's "Religious Affections," 2007

A Sincere and Pure Devotion to Christ: 100 Daily Meditations on 2 Corinthians 1–6, 2010

A Sincere and Pure Devotion to Christ: 100 Daily Meditations on 2 Corinthians 7–13, 2010

To the One Who Conquers: 50 Daily Meditations on the Seven Letters of Revelation 2–3, 2008

Tough Topics: Biblical Answers to 25 Challenging Questions, 2013

A Dozen Things
God Did with Your Sin

(And Three Things He'll Never Do)

Sam Storms

Foreword by Ray Ortlund

CROSSWAY®

WHEATON, ILLINOIS

A Dozen Things God Did with Your Sin (And Three Things He'll Never Do)

Copyright © 2022 by Sam Storms

Published by Crossway
        1300 Crescent Street
        Wheaton, Illinois 60187

Cover design: Spencer Fuller, Faceout Studios

Cover image: Christ on the Cross, Delacroix. Bridgeman Images

First printing 2022

Printed in the United States of America

Scripture quotations are from the ESV® Bible (The Holy Bible, English Standard Version®), copyright © 2001 by Crossway, a publishing ministry of Good News Publishers. Used by permission. All rights reserved.

All emphases in Scripture quotations have been added by the author.

Trade paperback ISBN: 978-1-4335-7660-7
ePub ISBN: 978-1-4335-7663-8
PDF ISBN: 978-1-4335-7661-4
Mobipocket ISBN: 978-1-4335-7662-1

Library of Congress Cataloging-in-Publication Data

Names: Storms, C. Samuel, 1951– author.
Title: A dozen things God did with your sin (and three things He'll never do) / Sam Storms.
Description: Wheaton, Illinois : Crossway, [2022] | Includes bibliographical references and indexes.
Identifiers: LCCN 2020049364 (print) | LCCN 2020049365 (ebook) | ISBN 9781433576607 (trade paperback) | ISBN 9781433576614 (pdf) | ISBN 9781433576621 (mobi) | ISBN 9781433576638 (epub)
Subjects: LCSH: Forgiveness of sin. | Forgiveness—Religious aspects—Christianity. | Conscience—Religious aspects—Christianity. | Sin—Biblical teaching. | God (Christianity)—Love.
Classification: LCC BT795 .S76 2022 (print) | LCC BT795 (ebook) | DDC 202/.2—dc23
LC record available at https://lccn.loc.gov/2020049364
LC ebook record available at https://lccn.loc.gov/2020049365

Crossway is a publishing ministry of Good News Publishers.

VP		31	30	29	28	27	26	25	24	23	22
14	13	12	11	10	9	8	7	6	5	4	3	2	1

Contents

Foreword

God is morally serious. Our consciences know that. But what our consciences struggle to believe is that God is also mercifully generous. And without confidence that God is both morally serious and mercifully generous, our consciences will never leave us in peace.

At the cross of Christ, God displayed his morally serious way to be mercifully generous. The Bible says that God is both "just and the justifier of the one who has faith in Jesus" (Rom. 3:26). God never cuts corners. He never trivializes our sin. But in God's mercy, Jesus lived the virtuous life for us that we haven't lived, and Jesus died the atoning death for us that we can't die. God upheld and enforced all his standards in our substitute, Jesus.

So where do we come in? Our part is to receive Jesus with the empty hands of faith. We can defy conscience. We can dare to trust Jesus. God *wants* us to. At the cross of Jesus, God's morally serious conscience and his mercifully generous heart combined *perfectly* to forgive us. God feels good about forgiving our sins. Which means we can feel good about being forgiven. Then, with our hearts at peace, we can finally get traction for newness of life.

But still, sometimes we find it hard to believe good news, don't we? The accusing voice within whispers, "Sure, go ahead and believe the gospel—up to a point. But what about *that* sin you committed, *that* betrayal, *that* hypocrisy—you at your worst? No, God is too disgusted with those sins! Maybe God will bless other people with peace and joy, because they haven't acted out the way you have. But you've sinned too far." Our merciless consciences would drag us back into anxiety, shame, and despair. That is why the Gallican Confession of 1559 counsels us to "*resolve* to be loved in Jesus Christ."[1]

In this new book, *A Dozen Things God Did with Your Sin (And Three Things He'll Never Do),* our dear friend Dr. Sam Storms helps us form that wise resolve. He helps us hear the gospel speaking into our deepest failures. He helps us step into new freedom of heart.

Pastor Storms is not glib and shallow. He understands the power of what he calls "a defiled conscience." He knows—I am going to quote Sam here—how these terrifying questions can eat at every one of us:

> *How can I come to God and be received by him and reconciled to him when I feel so dirty and unworthy? How can I be at peace with God when my conscience incessantly stabs at me with reminders of sin and lust and greed and ambition and selfishness and idolatry? How can I be assured that he really enjoys me as his child? Is there any hope that one day I might feel the affection God has for me?*

We need solid, biblical, satisfying answers to these profound questions of the heart. And that is where Sam guides us carefully

---

1 The French Confession of Faith, Apostles Creed (website), accessed August 10, 2021, https://apostles-creed.org/; emphasis added.

and thoughtfully. What awaits us in this book is a richer, fuller awareness of God's mercies that go down deeper than our very worst sin. And as we read all the way through no less than *a dozen things God mercifully did with our sin*, the layers of our disbelief can start peeling away, gospel relief can start entering in, and something of God's own joy can cheer our hearts.

Thank you, Sam, for serving desperate sinners like us with assurances from the Bible that are better than anything we could dream up on our own!

Now, as you are about to start Sam's book, I can't resist including one more thing. Let me leave you with a real-life illustration of how to fight for your own peace by the power of the gospel. Martin Luther, with his typical defiance, counseled us well:

> When the devil tells us we are sinners and therefore damned, we may answer, "Because you say I am a sinner, I will be righteous and saved." Then the devil will say, "No, you will be damned." And I will reply, "No, for I fly to Christ, who has given himself for my sins. Therefore, Satan, you will not prevail against me when you try to terrify me by telling me how great my sins are and try to reduce me to heaviness, distrust, despair, hatred, contempt and blasphemy. On the contrary, when you say I am a sinner, you give me armor and weapons against yourself, so that I can cut your throat with your own sword and tread you under my feet, for Christ died for sinners. . . . It is on his shoulders, not mine, that all my sins lie. . . . So when you say I am a sinner, you do not terrify me, but you comfort me immeasurably.[2]

2 Martin Luther, *Galatians*, ed. Alister McGrath and J. I. Packer (Wheaton, IL: Crossway Books, 1998), 40–41.

Even so, may God use this new book by Pastor Sam Storms to cheer all of our hearts with thoughts of Jesus big enough for our biggest regrets.

Ray Ortlund
Renewal Ministries
Nashville

Introduction

What Can Be Done about My
Dirty and Defiled Conscience?

THE ANGUISHED LOOK ON Marie's[1] face left no doubts about what was happening beneath the surface, in her heart. After several sessions meeting with me, she finally opened up. She winced every time I spoke of what the apostle Peter calls "joy inexpressible" and "full of glory" (1 Pet. 1:8). It got worse when I had her read Philippians 4:7 and she could barely mumble the words, "the peace that surpasses all understanding."

"Can you tell me," I asked, "why you struggle so painfully with the joy and peace that every Christian should experience? What prevents you from embracing and enjoying what Christ died to obtain? What is it that keeps you so far removed from such incredible blessings that God wants all of his children to receive?"

"My sin," came the brief but pointed reply. "My sin."

"But Marie, Jesus died in your place to suffer the penalty your sin required. And when you trusted him as Lord and Savior, you

---

1   The many individuals mentioned in this book are real, but their names have been changed.

were instantly and forever forgiven. All the guilt and shame of every sin you've ever committed or ever will commit is gone."

"I hear what you're saying. For heaven's sake, I read about it in my Bible almost every day. But the memory of my past sexual immorality still haunts me. And my life right now is a complete disaster. I can't seem to break free from the chains that enslave my heart. Will I ever be able to feel clean?"

Marie's struggle is all too familiar to many of you reading this book. And let's get one thing out of the way right up front. There are times when I feel exactly the same.

It's called a defiled conscience. I've been a Christian for over sixty years, but there are times when I fail to love my wife as I should or lose my temper or yield to certain temptations, and the piercing pain of condemnation strikes deeply into my soul. I hope that the frequency of my failures is decreasing the longer I know Jesus and the more I come to understand the majesty of his mercy to me. But all of us, both new believers and seasoned saints, will be confronted regularly with disquieting concerns that perhaps we've failed once too often and have pushed God to the limits of his grace.

There's no getting around the fact that this is why so many blood-bought, redeemed children of God continue to live bereft of the joy and peace that are two of the blessings Christ died to secure for us. We just can't bring ourselves to believe that God really loves us. How could he, when we have such a perpetual disdain for ourselves?

You know what your *conscience* is.[2] At times, it feels like our greatest enemy, and we wish it would just shut up! I'm talking about that spiritual dimension of the image of God indelibly imprinted

---

2   For a helpful discussion of what the New Testament means by "conscience," I highly recommend Andrew David Naselli and J. D. Crowley, *Conscience: What It Is, How to Train It, and Loving Those Who Differ* (Wheaton, IL: Crossway, 2016).

on our souls by which we have the capacity to feel guilt and conviction when we do wrong and joy and comfort when we do right. It is that facet or function of our souls by which our moral deeds, be they good or evil, are subjectively registered within. Everyone has a conscience, even non-Christians who have not yet been born again by the Spirit.

And everyone knows exactly what I'm talking about when I refer to those occasions when your conscience feels dirty. I'm talking about what you feel and sense deep within as you lie on your bed at night and reflect on the events of the day: the harsh words you spoke to your kids, the lie that you told your boss hoping to gain advancement, the pride you felt in your heart when someone praised your efforts.

I'm talking about what you feel and sense deep within when you wake up in the morning and lustful thoughts and sinful fantasies race through your mind. "Where did that come from," you wonder aloud? "What will God think of me now?" "How can I profess to be a Christian when my heart is besieged by such vile thoughts?"

I'm talking about what you feel and sense deep within when you navigate your way through the day without giving God so much as an afterthought. It's terrifyingly easy for us to take him for granted, much like we do the earth beneath our feet and the breath we breathe and the constant blinking of our eyes. The fact that we could treat God with such indifference is profoundly unsettling.

I'm talking about what you feel and sense deep within when you passed over in silence that incredible opportunity to share your faith and explain the gospel to a friend or coworker or neighbor. At the time, you convinced yourself you had a legitimate excuse to keep your mouth shut, but now all you can think about is the possibility of their eternal damnation. You wonder silently, *Can God really love a coward like me? Can he forgive one? How can I gain the sort of courage and boldness that will enable me to speak up next time?*

I'm talking about what you feel and sense deep within when you reflect on your life as a whole and all you see is one failure after another, one shattered dream after another, one devastating relationship after another, one sin after another. The anger that rises up in your heart is scary, as you so often end up blaming God for a life gone awry. *If he truly cared for me, why has everything gone haywire?* And then you begin to wonder whether God can actually be trusted with your life. With that, your conscience feels the sting of having doubted his goodness and competency.

I'm talking about what you feel and sense deep within when you consider how infinitely holy and pure and righteous God is and how immeasurably unholy and impure and unrighteous you are. *If God won't settle for anything less than sinless perfection, what possible hope do I have?*

I'm talking about what you feel and sense deep within as you try to figure out what you can do to bridge the gap between you and God, what you can say or promise or make up for so that he will love you and accept you. And then that random thought races through your head, *Give it up. It's too late. God gave up on you a long time ago, so go ahead and give up on him.*

I'm talking about what happens in your heart when you finally realize that not all the good works in the world or charitable gifts to the United Way or days spent serving in the soup kitchen at your city's rescue mission will enable you to measure up. The feeling of being utterly disqualified from citizenship in the kingdom of God swallows up whatever joy or confidence you once had.

"But What If . . ."

Let me dig a little deeper into the problem that this book is designed to address. All of us at some time or another, to varying degrees, struggle with the fear and the apprehension that perhaps God has not dealt fully and finally with our sin. We read in Scripture, just like Marie has done countless times, about the "joy" of our salvation and we've tasted it, a bit here and a bit there. But there is often this unshakable sense of condemnation that simply won't go away. It haunts us and taunts us and wants us to believe that there's simply no way God could look with love and approval on us.

Some of you react this way because you are plagued by an overly sensitive conscience. Even the slightest moral misstep squeezes from your heart what little joy you worked so hard to attain. You can barely hear anyone talk about the importance of obedience in the Christian life without concluding that you have failed miserably and are on the verge of being cast out. Others of you were raised in extremely religious and legalistic homes, and the church you attended only made matters worse with its oppressive, rigid, heavy-handed approach to Christian living. The result is that I've heard people say things like:

What if I push God into a corner with my repeated failures as a Christian? Won't he eventually get so fed up with me that he'll lash out in anger and cast me aside forever?

Or,

No one can possibly be that generous and gracious and forgiving, not even God. There has to be a limit to his patience, too, doesn't there?

Or,

I keep hearing this voice in my head that says forgiveness is for everyone else, but not me. After all, God's no idiot. He has to know the thoughts that enter my head and the words that come out of my mouth and the doubts and anger and frustration that I face every day.

Let me tell you why we think this way. Let me tell you why you aren't living in the fullness of the joy and peace and satisfaction in your relationship with God that you so desperately desire. It comes down to one thing and one thing only: *you and I have failed to believe what God himself says he has done with our sins.* What consumes us is what *we* have done by sinning. What ought to consume us is grateful meditation on what *God* has done with our sinning.

Most of us have been raised to think that anything that sounds too good to be true probably is. And nothing sounds better than freedom from that corrosive, gnawing anguish in our hearts that comes back each time we blow it. The problem is that our sin shouts so loudly that it often drowns out what feels like a barely faint promise from Scripture that God still loves us.

We're going to look at what God himself says he has done with our sin, as well as what he doesn't and never will do. But before we begin, one thing must be kept in mind. Everything I'm about to say about what God has done with your sin applies only to those who have repented and have run to the cross of Christ and have vested all their hope and faith and confidence in who Jesus Christ is and what he died and rose again from the grave to accomplish. If you do not know Christ as your Savior, I hope and pray what you read will persuade you that your only hope is in him. My aim, therefore, is to comfort and encourage Christians and to convict and convince non-Christians.

Eternal Union and Experiential Communion

There is one crucial issue that needs to be addressed before we go any further. Some people today say that God has forgiven only your sins of the past and those in the present that you have confessed, but he has not forgiven those sins that you will commit at some time in the future. He can't forgive them, so the argument goes, until you acknowledge, confess, and ask that he do so. At the other end of the theological spectrum are those who say that since God has finally and forever forgiven you of all your sins, you never need to confess them again, far less to ask for their forgiveness. Both of these views are misguided, largely because they fail to recognize the distinction between our *eternal union* with God and our *experiential communion* with him. In other words, they are both using the word *forgiveness* to refer to different realities. Let me explain.

When I refer to our eternal union with God, I'm talking about our standing in relation to our Creator. I'm talking about what is true of every born-again, Christ-trusting child of God. If you have truly been born of the Spirit, have repented of your sins, and look to Christ alone for your salvation, the following is true of you:

- You are now and forever will be in spiritual, loving, unbreakable union with God; you are in him and he is in you (Col. 1:2, 27).
- All your sins have been forgiven. That is to say, the guilt that is incurred from your sins, past, present, and future has been forever and finally wiped clean. This is why Paul says there is "no condemnation" for those who are in Christ Jesus by faith (Rom. 8:1).

- You are now and forever will be an adopted child of God (Gal. 4:4–7). This is your identity that defines both who you are and what awaits you on the other side of the grave.
- You are now and forever will be redeemed or ransomed from the condemning power of sin and guilt (Eph. 1:7).
- You are now and forever will be justified in God's sight, which is to say that through faith in Christ, God has imputed or reckoned to you the righteousness of Jesus and declared you to be perfectly acceptable in his sight, not because of what you have done but because of what Christ has done in living a sinless life and dying a substitutionary death for you (Rom. 3:28; 5:1).
- You are now and forever will be in spiritual union with Jesus Christ. Or, to use the words of the apostle Paul, you are by faith "in Christ" (Eph. 1:1).
- You are now and forever will be reconciled to God (2 Cor. 5:18–19).
- You are now and forever will be delivered or saved from the wrath of God. You will never face the threat of divine wrath, as Jesus has faced it, endured it, and exhausted it in himself on the cross (Rom. 5:9).
- You are now and forever will be seated together with Christ in heavenly places (Eph. 2:4–7).

This is what I mean when I speak of your eternal union with God. It is your position as a saved, redeemed, forgiven, justified, adopted child of God. It is eternal in the sense that it lasts forever. Nothing can change it, undo it, or reverse it. But these are also *nonexperiential* realities. In other words, you don't "feel" justification when it happens. You may feel an emotion of joy and gratitude because you are justified, but justification is not something that you experience in your body or your hormones or even in your emotions or affections. Nothing that happens in this life can affect your eternal union. Your obedience doesn't add to it and your disobedience doesn't detract from it. It is perfect and complete and final. But that doesn't mean your disobedience has no effect whatsoever on your relationship with God. Be patient. I'll get to that momentarily.

Our eternal union with Christ is what Paul had in mind when he reminded us that neither tribulation nor distress, neither persecution nor famine, neither nakedness nor danger nor sword can separate us from the love of God in Christ. That union between the believer and the Lord Jesus is unbreakable and indivisible. Neither death nor life, neither angels nor rulers, neither things present nor things to come, nor powers, neither height nor depth, nor anything else in all creation can break, undermine, diminish, or destroy our eternal union with God through faith in Jesus Christ (Rom. 8:35–39). So, our eternal union with God is our standing, our position, our eternal and unchanging relationship with our great triune God.

But our experiential communion is something different. Note first the contrast between the words *eternal* and *experiential*. The word *experiential* refers to what happens to us and in us now, in time, as each day passes. We *experience* the blessings of the indwelling Spirit. We *feel* the freedom of forgiveness. We *enjoy* the joy of knowing that God loves us. We *experience* the intimacy of walking in close relationship with Christ day in and day out. We can *tangibly sense* the power of the Spirit operating through us when we exercise the spiritual gifts he has given us. That is the difference between what is *eternal* and what is *experiential*.

We should next consider the difference between the words *union* and *communion*. The word *union* points to what is true of us in our relationship to God because of his grace. I am *united* with Christ through faith. I will always be in union with him. Christ's life is my life. His righteousness is my righteousness. I don't feel or experience this union, but I know it to be true because God says it is true.

But the word *communion* refers to what I can feel, sense, enjoy, and experience today and every day thereafter. Whereas my union with God never changes, my communion with him does. My union with God is unchanged by my sin, but my communion most certainly suffers. Whereas God is now and always will be my Father, my experience of that truth can go up and down. One day, I might enjoy his fatherly affection, but on another day, I may have lived in such a way that this enjoyment diminishes. My sonship didn't diminish. My status as God's child is unchanged. But my capacity to enjoy and feel the glory of being a child of God can be undermined by unrepentant sin.

Many have failed to properly differentiate between these two realities. They don't fully grasp the distinction between what is eternal and what is experiential, and they don't carefully differentiate between what is true of my union with God and my communion with him. Some so emphasize our eternal union with God that they think any reference to or emphasis on the experiential dynamics of our relationship with him is contrary to grace. Or worse still, it borders on legalism. To their way of thinking, to say that I "should" obey God, and that if I don't and remain unrepentant in sin I will not "experience" the sense of joy and peace that comes with being his child, is legalism. It is a failure to celebrate grace.

No, it isn't.

Now, is it possible for people to live as though the daily experiential disobedience of the Christian can undermine or overturn his or her eternal union? Yes. But it can't. That's the glory of grace. But it is equally wrong to think that our daily experiential disobedience has no effect on our ability to enjoy God's presence and power. It most assuredly can, and does.

If you will keep clearly in your mind this difference between your eternal union with God and your experiential communion with him, you'll be able to make sense of all that follows.

The condemnation that comes with my sin and guilt has been forever removed because Christ took it upon himself. When it comes to my eternal union with God, I have been fully and finally forgiven of all my sins—past, present, and future. I need never again ask for forgiveness for sins when it comes to my salvation or my eternal union with God or my deliverance from guilt and the divine wrath it evokes. But when it comes to my sanctification or my daily experiential communion with God, I need to confess and receive forgiveness in order that I might fully enjoy and delight in and be satisfied with all that God has done for me in Christ.

This distinction explains why I can speak so confidently of what God has done with our sins and at the same time encourage Christian men and women to humbly confess their sins and seek God's forgiveness and the restoration of sweet fellowship. People who have opposed the idea that believers should continue to confess their sins and seek forgiveness do so, largely, because they are thinking of our eternal union with the Lord. When it comes to that aspect of our relationship to God, all sins have forever been set aside, forgiven, cast into the sea, and blotted out. We need only ask God once for forgiveness from our sins in order to be saved. When it comes to the establishment of that unbreakable union with

God, his forgiveness comes once and for all time. It is singular and unrepeatable. But when we are addressing the daily experiential failures that disrupt and undermine our capacity to enjoy intimacy with the Lord, confession is a daily duty, and forgiveness is always available (see 1 John 1:8–9).

In the pages that follow, you will see this issue come up again and again. My primary concern is with what God has done with your sin in order to establish that irrevocable eternal union with himself. So, when you come across statements that refer to the urgency of confessing our sins and renewing felt fellowship with the Father, be assured that I am not speaking out of both sides of my mouth. In the former case, I have in mind our standing as justified, redeemed, fully forgiven children of God. In the latter, I am talking about the experiential impact of unrepentant sin on your ability to rest in your eternal relationship with the Lord and to enjoy him on a daily basis.

Here is the bottom line. The frequent disruption of and damage done to our experiential communion with God often leads us to question the reality of our eternal union with him. And it is the rock-solid assurance that God has dealt finally and forever with the guilt of our sin that, in turn, empowers our capacity on a daily basis to enjoy what it means to be a blood-bought child of God. Well, I'm getting ahead of myself. So let's get started.

1

How Hebrews Helps

SOMETIMES PROFOUND TRUTHS are tucked away in obscure and neglected places. That is certainly the case with what we see in Hebrews 9:13–14. My guess is that many of you have never given much consideration to this passage, especially given its place in a book of the New Testament whose language and imagery are so seemingly out of touch with our technologically sophisticated world. And yet I am persuaded that there is immeasurably powerful and practical truth in this one text. In fact, there is a sense in which this passage is a banner over the whole of this book you are reading. There we read,

> For if the blood of goats and bulls, and the sprinkling of defiled persons with the ashes of a heifer, sanctify for the purification of the flesh, how much more will the blood of Christ, who through the eternal Spirit offered himself without blemish to God, purify our conscience from dead works to serve the living God. (Heb. 9:13–14)

I can think of no more pressing and urgent need than to have our consciences purified so that we might love and serve and live for God and his glory. So, what do you do when your conscience feels dirty or when your soul feels soiled?

Here's what's remarkable. As different as our world is today from the world of the Old Testament when the tabernacle still stood and the rituals of the Mosaic Law were still in force, the most fundamental problem of the human heart is the same. The most basic need of every man and woman remains unchanged. In spite of our technological advances and the internet and our breaking of the genetic code and the existence of automobiles and deodorant and indoor plumbing, the most basic and fundamental and pressing need of your heart and of mine is no different from what it was for those Israelites who lived during Old Testament times when the tabernacle and later the temple were standing and in full operation.

And what is that problem? A dirty conscience. A defiled spirit. A stained soul. A heart that feels wicked and wayward and for all of its efforts can't seem to make its way back to God.

I find it fascinating that even after you spend an evening parked in front of the television with your family, staring at your computer, drowning your pain in alcohol, reading a book, or checking the results of movement in the stock market, you are still wrestling with one core struggle and seeking an answer to one essential question:

> *How can I come to God and be received by him and reconciled to him when I feel so dirty and unworthy? How can I be at peace with God when my conscience incessantly stabs at me with reminders of sin and lust and greed and ambition and selfishness and idolatry? How can I be assured that he really enjoys me as his child? Is there any hope that one day I might feel the affection God has for me?*

What we find in Hebrews 9 is the only answer, the only solution to that problem. The only thing that will purify your conscience so that you can enjoy God and know that he enjoys you is "the blood of Christ" (v. 14). All that the offerings, sacrifices, and furnishings of the Old Testament temple could do was to cleanse the person outwardly so that he or she could join in with the rest of God's people in worship and prayer. These offerings and sacrifices cleansed only their bodies, removing ceremonial defilement and qualifying them for life in the community of God's people.

But their consciences were never fully and finally and forever cleansed of the defiling power of guilt that was the result of sin.

Virtually everything associated with the Old Testament tabernacle and its furnishings, together with the elaborate instructions that governed the offering of "the blood of goats and bulls" (v. 13) were designed to serve as a visual sermon declaring the holiness of God. The necessity for continual washings and cleansing of everyone and everything that entered the tabernacle was a constant reminder that God's holiness is of such a nature that only the perfect and pure are acceptable to him.

The tabernacle and everything in it were also daily reminders not just of God's holiness but of man's sinfulness. Everything there shouted out, "Stay away! Do not draw near! If you come near to God, you will die!" That is why access to God's presence was restricted to only one man, the high priest, on one day of the year, and then only if he brought to the altar a sacrifice of blood for both himself and the people.

But most important of all, the tabernacle and everything in it pointed to the coming of the person and work of Jesus Christ. May I remind you that when John the apostle described the incarnation of the Son of God, the entrance into human flesh and into the life of this world of the second person of the Trinity, he wrote, "And the Word became flesh and dwelt among us, and we have seen his glory, glory as of the only Son from the Father, full of grace and truth" (John 1:14). And the word translated "dwelt" is more literally "tabernacled"! The mercy and grace and forgiveness and glory and beauty that the tabernacle embodied has now come to us fully and finally in the person of Jesus!

Set Free from the Bondage of Religion

The author of Hebrews arrives at his glorious conclusion in 9:14. Here he declares that over against the blood of bulls and goats that could provide only external ceremonial cleansing, the blood of our Savior cleanses our consciences and brings us the final and full forgiveness of sins.

And from what is our conscience purified or cleansed? "Dead works" (v. 14). He has in mind everything we have ever done thinking that it would redeem our souls; everything we've ever said hoping that our words would turn away God's wrath; everything we ever gave, sacrificed, promised, turned away from thinking that it would put our conscience, heart, and mind at rest. They are "dead" because they have no power to reconcile us to God. They are "dead" because they come from hearts that are devoid of spiritual life. They are "dead" because they leave us feeling hopeless that anything could ever set us free from the condemning power of sin and guilt.

And it is only from a pure conscience, one made right and clean by the blood of Christ, that we can then serve God and love him and glorify him in the way that he originally designed when he created us.

Do you want another word in place of "dead works"? I'll give you one: *religion*! Religion is the attempt to motivate people to do "good works" on the basis of their *feelings* of guilt. The gospel calls people to "good works" on the basis of the *forgiveness* of guilt! Religion says, "You're obviously feeling guilty and dirty and defiled. So here's what you need to do: go to work for God! Give more. Pray more. Serve more. Do more."

The gospel says, "The problem isn't that you *feel* guilty. The problem is that you *are* guilty! So here's what you need to do: receive by faith the work God in Christ has already done for you!"

Are you still paralyzed by a dirty conscience? Does that feeling of moral stain on your soul leave you in despair and hopelessness? There is only one solution, only one thing that can cleanse and make you whole: the blood of Jesus Christ shed at the cross for sinners like you and me.

Charles Simeon was born in 1759 and died in 1836. He remembered well his conversion to Christ. It happened as he read about what happened on the Day of Atonement when the high priest laid his hands on the scapegoat, symbolizing the transfer of guilt from the people of Israel to the sacrificial offering. "The thought came into my mind," said Simeon, "'What, may I transfer all my guilt to another? Has God provided an Offering for me, that I may lay my sins on his head?' Then, God willing, I will not bear them on my soul one moment longer. Accordingly I sought to lay my sins upon the sacred head of Jesus."[1]

You can do the same today and be cleansed and set free from a dirty conscience forever.

That's what this book is all about. But it won't come easily. That isn't because there is some deficiency in what God has provided for us in Jesus Christ. It's because *sin has hardwired us for*

---

1 Cited by F. F. Bruce, *The Epistle to the Hebrews* (Grand Rapids, MI: Eerdmans, 1973), 194n56.

self-punishment. Our instinctive and initial response to personal failure is to demand from ourselves something that can never remove the stain of guilt. All of our promises and good intentions and self-help formulas, as well as the many ways we seek to inflict pain, be it physical or emotional, fail to secure for our souls what they so desperately need. Not even the multitude of sacrifices we make, together with all manner of self-deprivation and new rules we impose on our lives, can atone for our sins. Grace is simply too big of a pill for many to swallow.

Over the years, God has brought to my attention several young ladies who sought relief from a defiled conscience through cutting. In one case, while in my office at the church, I had to wrestle the razor blade from her hand before she could slice her wrists. In another, a student of mine at Wheaton College had to withdraw from school to seek intense counseling to find freedom from the compulsion to harm herself. More recently, I rejoiced when a precious young lady handed me a pack of box cutters, a token of the fact that she was eight years removed from the last time she had disfigured her flesh in an attempt to make things right with God.

I'm not suggesting that I have uncovered the underlying motivation in all those who struggle with the temptation to self-harm. It is a massively complex problem. But I can assure you that in many instances, there is the ungodly belief that the shed blood of Jesus on the cross wasn't enough to wash one's soul clean of the defiling presence of guilt. *Mine too is needed.* Or for others, it seems to be the only successful way to silence the silent screams of a desperate conscience that longs to be free and forgiven.

Regardless of what your greatest struggle or sin may be, our only hope is to listen closely to what the Bible says God has done with our sin, and to submit to this truth by faith in Jesus Christ.

2

He Laid Your Sin upon His Son

OF THE DOZEN THINGS God has done with your sin, none is more foundational to securing for you the joy and peace of a clean conscience than the fact that God has laid your sin upon his Son. In fact, all of the eleven remaining things that God has done with your sin are grounded in this one. Most of the other eleven truths we will explore are images or metaphors or analogies designed to drive home the glorious truth that because of God's having laid our sin on his Son, we are forgiven. In other words, it is precisely, and for no other reason, that God has judged Jesus in your place, as your atoning substitute, that we can even speak of the possibility of forgiveness. As a result of its foundational nature, this chapter inevitably needs more space than the other eleven things God has done with our sin.

The Glory of Penal Substitutionary Atonement

I should probably begin with defining my terms, as I suspect some of you are scratching your heads when you look at the subheading of this chapter. *Penal? Substitutionary? Atonement?* What does that mean and why is it glorious?

I'll unpack these terms in greater detail as we move forward, but for now, a brief explanation is in order. Our sin warrants a penalty. We call it punishment or judgment. That penalty is eternal damnation. Each of us is a hell-deserving sinner. That is the penalty we incur when we commit cosmic treason against God by defying his will and living in rebellious unbelief. Our only hope of escaping this penalty is if there is a qualified and willing substitute to take our place and exhaust the demands of divine law that are against us. This is why we speak of the death of Jesus as a *penal substitution.* He suffers the penalty in our place. The result is that when we lay hold of this truth by faith alone and invest our hope of reconciliation with God in who Jesus is and what he has done on the cross, *atonement* is made. We are made "at-one" with God. Does this not merit the acclamation, *glory?* The glory of the atonement as found in Christ's penal substitutionary death is the heart of the biblical gospel. We're now ready to dig a little deeper into this marvelous truth.

So, what do the biblical authors have in mind when they say things such as we find in Isaiah 53 and 1 Peter 2? Let's begin with the Old Testament text.

He was despised and rejected by men,
    a man of sorrows and acquainted with grief;
and as one from whom men hide their faces
    he was despised, and we esteemed him not.

Surely he has borne our griefs
    and carried our sorrows;
yet we esteemed him stricken,
    smitten by God, and afflicted.

But he was pierced for our transgressions;
    he was crushed for our iniquities;
upon him was the chastisement that brought us peace,
    and with his wounds we are healed.
All we like sheep have gone astray;
    we have turned—every one—to his own way;
and the Lord has laid on him
    the iniquity of us all. (Isa. 53:3–6)

The most explicit assertion in this paragraph is found in verse 6, where the prophet speaks of the Messiah, the suffering servant, as the one on whom "the Lord" (i.e., God the Father) has "laid . . . the iniquity of us all." Other statements speak of much the same thing: "we esteemed him stricken, smitten by God, and afflicted" (v. 4). Again, "he was pierced for our transgressions; he was crushed for our iniquities" (v. 5a). It was "upon him" that the chastisement that brought us peace was laid (v. 5b). Twice more, Isaiah declares that "he shall bear their [your!] iniquities" (v. 11) and "he bore the sin of many" (v. 12).

The apostle Peter had much the same in mind when he said that Jesus "himself bore our sins in his body on the tree" (1 Pet. 2:24). We should also consider Leviticus 16, the Day of Atonement, and the scapegoat, where the Hebrew word *kipper* appears sixteen times and often refers to the propitiation of God's wrath through the offering of a substitutionary animal sacrifice, cleansing the people from their sin. The words of Jesus himself most certainly cannot be ignored. He spoke of the purpose of his coming as a giving of his life "as a ransom for many" (Matt. 20:28; Mark 10:45). If through faith in who Jesus is and what he has done we are delivered from condemnation (John 3:18), it can be only because he himself endured that condemnation in our place. Indeed, a rejection of Jesus means that "the wrath of God remains" on the individual sinner (v. 36). Simply put, either Jesus bears the wrath of God in your place or you bear it yourself.

So how does one escape the wrath and condemnation of God due to our sin? Paul affirms that the hope of "redemption" (Rom. 3:24) comes through Jesus Christ, "whom God put forward as a propitiation by his blood" (v. 25). As much as some wish to evade the clear meaning of this term,[1] the noun *hilasterion* and the verbal form *hilaskomai* mean, respectively, "propitiation" and "to propitiate"—that is, to satisfy or to placate (cf. Heb. 2:17; 1 John 2:2; 4:10). The focus of this action is God himself and the manifestation of his wrath against sin (see Rom. 5:8–10; 8:1–3).

Other expressions are used to communicate the same truth, such as Paul's statement that "Christ redeemed us from the curse of the law by becoming a curse for us" (Gal. 3:13). Divine justice and its expression in divine wrath against sin, to use Paul's words, call for the reckoning or "counting" of our trespasses "against" us (2 Cor. 5:19). So how is it that, instead, you and I are forgiven the guilt of these wicked deeds? The answer of the apostle, in verse 21, is that God "made him [Jesus] to be sin" on our behalf. Don't ever think that the love of God means that the wrath of God was ignored. Because God is just and righteous, there must be a reckoning or "counting" of trespasses. But because God and his Son are loving and gracious, the *counting* or *imputing* and the punishment it entailed fell on Christ.

---

1   For the best treatment of propitiation, see Leon Morris, *The Apostolic Preaching of the Cross*, 3rd ed. (Grand Rapids, MI: Eerdmans, 1972). If Morris's discussion proves a bit too challenging, I highly recommend J. I. Packer's explanation in *Knowing God* (Downers Grove, IL: IVP, 1993), 179–99.

This counting or reckoning of our sins against Jesus is what Paul means in 2 Corinthians 5:21 when he speaks of Jesus being "made to be sin" on our behalf. Paul is talking about the liability to suffer the penal consequences of the law. Our guilt, incurred because of our trespasses, has been imputed to Jesus so that we, through faith in his sufferings on our behalf, might have his righteousness imputed to us! Or, as Peter puts it, Christ "suffered once for sins, the righteous for [that is, in the place of, as a substitute for] the unrighteous" (1 Pet. 3:18).

When Paul says that God "made" Jesus "to be sin" he does not mean that Jesus in some mysterious manner actually committed sins in our stead. That would be senseless, and would render Jesus disqualified from making a satisfactory atonement on our behalf. What Paul means is that Jesus was legally reckoned to be guilty of the sins we commit and, therefore, subject to the divine penalty that all sin merits.

From these and other texts, we have but one conclusion: "If God did not punish his Son in my place, I am not saved from my greatest peril, the wrath of God."[2] We have only one hope and it is "that the infinite wisdom of God might make a way for the love of God to satisfy the wrath of God so that I might become a son of God."[3] How, then, might we define penal substitution? Put simply, "The doctrine of penal substitution states that God gave himself in the person of his Son to suffer instead of us the death, punishment and curse due to fallen humanity as the penalty for sin."[4]

---

2 John Piper, foreword to Steve Jeffery, Mike Ovey, and Andrew Sach, *Pierced for Our Transgressions: Rediscovering the Glory of Penal Substitution* (Nottingham: Inter-Varsity Press, 2007), 14.

3 Piper, foreword to Jeffery, Ovey, and Sach, *Pierced for Our Transgressions*, 14.

4 Jeffery, Ovey, and Sach, *Pierced for Our Transgressions*, 21.

There simply can be no Christian gospel apart from the truth that Jesus Christ has endured and suffered in himself, on the cross, the wrath of God due to sinners, thereby propitiating or satisfying said wrath on behalf of those for whom he died. This is what I mean by saying that God has "laid" our sin upon Christ, his Son.

When you struggle to know where the guilt and condemnation that you and I deserved have gone, God has laid them upon his Son. This is the doctrine of imputation, according to which the guilt of our sin has been transferred, or legally reckoned, to Jesus. He is accounted as guilty in our place, and thus incurs the penalty that such guilt requires.

Answering Objections to Penal Substitutionary Atonement

There are several excellent defenses of penal substitutionary atonement that go into considerable detail in responding to objections. I encourage you to consult them.[5] Here I will briefly address some of the more common arguments.

Some object by pointing out that penal substitution is not the only model of atonement. But no one ever said it was. We must

5   The literature defining and defending penal substitution is massive. Among the many treatments, I have found the best to be Jeffery, Ovey, and Sach, *Pierced for Our Transgressions*; J. I. Packer, "What Did the Cross Achieve? The Logic of Penal Substitution," *Tyndale Bulletin* 25 (1974): 3–45; D. A. Carson, "Atonement in Romans 3:21–26: God Presented Him as a Propitiation," in *The Glory of the Atonement: Biblical, Historical & Practical Perspectives, Essays in Honor of Roger Nicole*, ed. Charles E. Hill and Frank A. James III (Downers Grove, IL: IVP Academic, 2004), 119–39; Garry J. Williams, "Penal Substitution: A Response to Recent Criticisms," *Journal of the Evangelical Theological Society* 50, no. 1 (March 2007): 71–86; J. I. Packer and Mark Dever, *In My Place Condemned He Stood: Celebrating the Glory of the Atonement* (Wheaton, IL: Crossway Books, 2007); Morris, *The Apostolic Preaching of the Cross*; Paul Wells, *Cross Words: The Biblical Doctrine of the Atonement* (Ross-Shire: Christian Focus, 2006); Robert L. Dabney, *Christ Our Penal Substitute* (Harrisonburg: Sprinkle Publications, 1978); David Peterson, ed., *Where Wrath and Mercy Meet: Proclaiming the Atonement Today* (Carlisle: Paternoster Press, 2001); and John R. W. Stott, *The Cross of Christ* (Leicester: IVP, 1986).

keep in mind that all of the many theories or models of the atonement are in some sense true, at least in terms of what they affirm. Yes, the death of Jesus exerts a "moral influence" on us, insofar as it provides an "example" for how we are to respond to unjustified suffering (see 1 Pet. 2:21–23). Yes, God is the supreme "moral governor" of the created realm, whose commitment to the interests of public law and order was vindicated and displayed in the death of Jesus (see Rom. 3:25–26). Yes, the death of Jesus conquered evil and was designed to undo the works of Satan (see 1 John 3:8) and liberate those held captive by him. Yes, the death of Jesus was designed to restore in mankind the *imago Dei* (image of God) so horribly defaced (but not destroyed) by the fall into sin. Yes, we see in the death of Jesus his voluntary submission to weakness and identification with the outcast and marginalized of society. But all of these things are true only because his death was preeminently a dying in the place of sinners, enduring in himself (body and soul) and thereby propitiating (see Rom. 3:25; 1 John 2:1–2) the wrath of a righteous God.

Satan was defeated, the *imago Dei* was restored, the effects of Adam's fall were reversed, God's righteous rule was vindicated, and an inspirational example of love and self-sacrifice was provided because Jesus, as an expression of the incomparable love of God for sinners (Rom. 5:8), voluntarily suffered the penal consequences of the law of God, the just for the unjust, dying our death, bearing "our sins in his body on the tree" (1 Pet. 2:24). So long as the penal substitutionary sacrifice of Jesus is retained as foundational and fundamental to what happened on Calvary, we should joyfully celebrate and give thanks for all else that it accomplished.

Some critics argue that penal substitution diminishes the significance of Jesus's life and resurrection. But virtually all of those who advocate penal substitution have always insisted that Christ's entire life on earth was part of his atoning work. Both the active and passive obedience of Jesus are essential to his redemptive work. Our Lord's faithful obedience to the law and his sinless submission to the will of his Father are inseparable from the sufficiency of his atoning sacrifice. And if Jesus was not raised from the dead, his death is of no more benefit to us than that of the two thieves crucified on his left and his right.

I've also heard it said that penal substitution is unable to address the real needs of human culture and the desires of the human heart. In other words, critics argue that this model of atonement will not gain acceptance in large parts of the modern world because it fails to address our perceived needs or cannot be understood by those in different social settings. It is true, of course, that penal substitution may be less readily grasped in certain cultures where its foundational ideas are absent. "However, this does not make it 'unintelligible'; it just means that the task of explanation may be more difficult."[6] Our church recently sent a young couple and their two children to Japan to join another ministry with a view to church planting. Japan's honor-shame culture will make it exceedingly more difficult to explain the gospel to people in that nation, but that is no reason to alter, diminish, or reframe the essence of the good news. It simply places a greater burden than usual on those who are committed to making Christ known in that largely unreached nation.

One of the more ridiculous—indeed, blasphemous—objections is that penal substitution lends credence to the charge that the cross is tantamount to "cosmic child abuse." This sort of inflammatory and essentially wicked rhetoric needs to be defused. Penal

6 Jeffery, Ovey, and Sach, *Pierced for Our Transgressions*, 222.

substitution differs in countless ways from child abuse. I'll mention only three.

First, according to this understanding of atonement, Jesus voluntarily and willingly went to his death, knowing full well what was entailed by it (John 10:11, 17–18). Child abuse, on the other hand, involves inflicting pain upon an unwilling victim, or exploiting a person who is unable to understand fully what is happening.

Second, according to penal substitution, Jesus died to glorify both himself and the Father, as well as to save his people from their sins (see John 17:1–5; Rom. 3:21–26). Child abuse is carried out solely for the perverse gratification of the abuser.

And this brings me to the third difference: namely, the character and intent of God the Father. His giving of the Son was motivated by love and a desire to restore his fallen creation (see John 3:16). Likewise, the Son "loves us and has freed us from our sins by his blood" (Rev. 1:5). Much more can be said in response to this scurrilous accusation, such as the explicit testimony of Isaiah 53:10 that "it was the will of the LORD to crush him; / he has put him to grief." One should also consider the role of the Father in the Son's death as stated in Acts 2:23, 3:18, and 4:27–28.

Related to this is the objection that the notion of "redemptive violence" is a myth. In other words, violence doesn't work. It only compounds the problem. But Jesus was fully aware that a violent death awaited him in Jerusalem and set himself to pursue that course (Mark 10:33–34). If the critics of penal substitution are right, then Jesus made a colossal mistake. Let's also not forget that the entire Old Testament sacrificial system was violent, yet had profound redemptive benefits. Finally, the violence entailed in Jesus' death differs greatly from how we see it manifest in other settings. Jesus died voluntarily (John 10:11, 17–18) and selflessly, motivated by love for the glory of his Father and the salvation of those for whom he suffered. And Jesus's death, unlike other expressions of violence, was in fulfillment of justice, not a violation of it.

Another oft-heard objection to penal substitution is that it is inconsistent with principles of justice, for how can an innocent man be punished for the guilt of others? Guilt, say the critics, cannot be transferred. Needless to say, the biblical authors disagree! We must remember that penal substitution does not argue that a transfer of guilt takes place between people unrelated to each other. Those whose guilt is imputed to Christ are united to him. In other words, "union with Christ explains how the innocent could be justly punished—he is judged for others' sins, which, by virtue of their union with him, become his. Conversely, it explains also how the guilty can be justly acquitted—believers are one with the innocent Lord Jesus Christ, and so his life of perfect righteousness is rightly imputed to us."[7]

A related objection is that penal substitution implicitly denies that God forgives sin, for if Christ suffers for our transgressions, there is nothing left for God to forgive. But this fails to see that the reason penal substitution does not deny that God forgives sin is precisely because it is God himself, in the person of his Son, Jesus Christ, who pays the debt we owe. It may well be true that in the relationship between human beings, receiving payment and offering forgiveness are mutually exclusive, but the same does not obtain in God's relationship with his creatures. God did "what no human creditor could do, even in principle: he received payment by giving himself in the person of his Son to take our human na-

---

7   Jeffery, Ovey, and Sach, *Pierced for Our Transgressions*, 244.

ture and suffer the punishment we deserve. In this way he himself repaid the debt of all who are in Christ, paving the way for us to receive his forgiveness."[8]

It is occasionally objected that penal substitution doesn't work because Christ didn't suffer the equivalent that was due us. In other words, how could an infinite punishment be borne in a finite time? This is similar to the objection raised against eternal conscious punishment in hell. Some protest by saying that a finite number of sins committed in time is hardly deserving of an eternity of retribution in hell. But we must remember that these so-called finite sins were perpetrated against an infinitely holy and immeasurably beautiful God who is deserving of perfect obedience and unfailing worship. In other words, the duration of punishment in hell should not be determined by the length of time or the quantity of sins committed, but by the degree of honor and glory of the one against whom sin is perpetrated. Likewise, it is the infinite and unfathomable dignity and honor of Jesus Christ that determines the quality and efficacy of his sufferings, not the duration of time within which he endured them. Thus, Christ's suffering, although of limited length, was still of unfathomable and immeasurable value because of who he is. His infinite worth made his agonies on the cross infinitely efficacious. It is the spiritual, moral, and majestic quality of the Lord Jesus Christ that matters and makes his suffering sufficient to atone for our sin, not the length of time that he remained on the tree.

Yet another baseless protest is that penal substitution is in danger of severing the Godhead, pitting one member of the Trinity against another. But there is nothing wrong in principle with saying that

8 Jeffery, Ovey, and Sach, *Pierced for Our Transgressions*, 265.

one person of the Trinity does something 'to' another. The Father "sends" the Son, "loves" the Son, "glorifies" the Son, and so on. The Son, in turn, sent the Spirit whose primary goal is to shed light on the glory and splendor of the Son (John 16:7–15). Why is it so difficult to envision a scenario in which, by voluntary agreement, the Father "punishes" the Son in the place of those for whom he dies?

One more objection, related to the Christian life, is the bizarre suggestion that penal substitution causes people to live in constant fear of God. Of course, the body of Christ could do with a little (a lot of?) healthy reverential fear of God. And might it be that a persistent fear of God comes from a neglect or even denial of penal substitution? When people read Scripture and repeatedly encounter the reality of divine wrath, only then to find penal substitution ignored in our pulpits, "is it any wonder they are left with a troubled conscience? For if God's holy wrath was not endured by Christ in our place, it remains upon us,"[9] and that, dear friend, is certainly good grounds for fear.

There are other underlying reasons why penal substitution is being attacked in our day. One could point to: (1) the changing view of God, one that denies wrath as a personal attribute (wrath is not what God feels, so we are being told, but is simply the impersonal moral consequence that invariably follows upon evil choices); (2) the dislike of the emphasis on individual salvation in which Christianity is viewed as primarily about me getting my sins forgiven so I can go to heaven when I die; this is tied up with a disdain for an escapist mentality that ignores earthly problems for a pie-in-the-sky, by-and-by religion such that social justice is

---

9 Jeffery, Ovey, and Sach, *Pierced for Our Transgressions*, 320.

ignored; (3) the reaction against anything associated with or looking like the older fundamentalism; and finally (4) the growing emphasis on passivism as a broad approach to life, together with a reaction against anything remotely connected with violence.

Simply put, everything else that God has done with our sin is the fruit of this one incredibly gracious and glorious act of God. Jesus voluntarily offered himself to be your substitute, to die in your place on the cross, to suffer the judgment you deserved. The Father, in turn, reckoned Jesus to be guilty of your sins and thus liable to the punishment you deserved. He accounted or imputed Jesus as guilty, even though he was innocent.[10]

Peter and Paul on Penal Substitution

So much more could be written about Christ's death as a penal substitutionary sacrifice in which he endured, absorbed, and exhausted the wrath of God that you and I deserved. But I will limit myself to a few additional comments from the apostles Peter and

10 In response to those who suggest that penal substitution was not understood or taught in the church until Anselm in the eleventh century, the evidence suggests otherwise. Among the many advocates of penal substitution, I point to Justin Martyr (c. 100–165), Eusebius of Caesarea (c. 275–339), Hilary of Poitiers (c. 300–368), Athanasius (c. 300–373), Gregory of Nazianzus (c. 330–390), Ambrose of Milan (339–397), John Chrysostom (c. 350–407), Augustine (354–430), Cyril of Alexandria (375–444), and Gregory the Great (c. 540–604). Other significant figures who understood the atonement in this way include Thomas Aquinas (c. 1225–1274), John Calvin (1509–1564), Francis Turretin (1623–1687), John Bunyan (1628–1688), John Owen (1616–1683), George Whitefield (1714–1770), Charles Spurgeon (1834–1892), D. Martyn Lloyd-Jones (1899–1981), as well as John Stott (1921–2011) and J. I. Packer (1926–2020). These are representative thinkers who represent only a small fraction of those who have embraced the truth of penal substitution. It's also important to remember that even when the vocabulary with which we typically define penal substitution is not found in the writings of a particular figure, the concept or idea may still be present. For a complete discussion, see Jeffery, Ovey, and Sach, *Pierced for our Transgressions*, 161–204; Michael J. Vlach, "Penal Substitution in Church History," *The Master's Seminary Journal* 20, no. 2 (Fall 2009):199–214; and Garry J. Williams, "Penal substitutionary atonement in the Church Fathers," *Evangelical Quarterly* 83, no. 3 (2011), 195–216.

Paul. We'll look first at what Peter says in 1 Peter 2:24–25 and then at Paul's comments in 2 Corinthians 5.

Peter's Perspective

"Rock of Ages" is one of those older hymns of the Christian faith that one rarely hears anymore, even in churches that are more traditional in their approach to worship. It was written by Augustus Toplady (d. 1776). I've always been fascinated by the lyrics in the first verse:

> Rock of Ages, cleft for me,
> Let me hide myself in Thee;
> Let the water and the blood,
> From Thy wounded side which flowed,
> *Be of sin the double cure;*
> *Save from wrath and make me pure.* (emphasis added)

It's those last two lines that I have in mind: "Be of sin the double cure; save from wrath and make me pure." Toplady is obviously trying to tell us that, in his view, sin has caused us two massive problems, both of which are overcome by the redemptive work of Christ on the cross. We need, says Toplady, a *double* cure from the debilitating and destructive power of sin. First, we need to be saved from divine wrath: "Be of sin the double cure; *save from wrath* and make me pure." In other words, sin has exposed us to divine wrath. We have violated—in thought, word, and deed—the will of God. We are alienated from our Creator. We have incurred the penalty for breaking the law of God: namely, suffering the wrath of God. The appeal in the hymn is for the blood of Christ to save us from divine wrath and judgment.

But then Toplady makes a second appeal. "Be of sin the double cure; save from wrath and make me pure." It isn't enough to be delivered from the penalty of sin. We must also be set free from the power of sin. We need the redemptive work of Christ, through the Spirit, to be applied to us in such a way that we find strength and power to overcome the presence of sin and to resist temptation and to grow in likeness and conformity to the image of Jesus Christ.

Both of these dimensions of the work of Christ on the cross are in view in Peter's first epistle. There we read,

> He himself bore our sins in his body on the tree, that we might die to sin and live to righteousness. By his wounds you have been healed. For you were straying like sheep, but have now returned to the Shepherd and Overseer of your souls. (1 Pet. 2:24–25)

When Peter says that Jesus "bore our sins in his body on the tree," he has in view the fact that Jesus was regarded by God the Father as guilty of every sin you've ever committed. Jesus was reckoned as the one who deserved the punishment that should have fallen on you and me. But by God's grace it fell, instead, on him. By enduring the wrath of God in our place, as our substitute, we have been saved from divine wrath, just as Toplady described it in his hymn. Those who believe in Jesus Christ will never suffer the wrath of God for one reason and for one reason only: it is because Jesus has suffered and satisfied the wrath of God in our place.

Now here's the problem. There are many who believe that if by Christ's death we are forever set free from the wrath and judgment of God, we will take advantage of that fact and live however we please. We will immerse ourselves in sinful self-indulgence. After all, if I can never endure God's wrath because Christ has endured it in my place, what difference does it make how I live? Why should I bother worrying about temptation? Who cares if I watch pornography or commit fornication or become addicted to alcohol or cheat on my wife or steal or gossip or lie or allow my life to be conformed to what the world says is the way to live?

Peter's perspective is utterly opposite to this. He couldn't be any more explicit: Christ died for you and bore the punishment you deserved and endured God's wrath for sin precisely so that you might find the strength and motivation and incentive for saying no to sin in your daily life and yes to righteousness and purity and godliness. In fact, Peter says it three times in this paragraph.

He first said back in 2:21, "Christ also suffered for you, leaving you an example, so that you might follow in his steps." One of the primary goals in his death for us was to enable us to live like him. He walked a certain path. He has left for us spiritual and moral footprints. "Walk in them," says God. "Live like Jesus." And of course, one of the ways in which we do that is by not retaliating against those who treat us unfairly or persecute us unjustly.

He says it a second time in verse 24a: "He himself bore our sins in his body on the tree, that we might die to sin and live to righteousness." Another of the primary goals in his death for us was to make it possible for us to be as dead people when it comes to sin. Here's the analogy he has in view. With regard to sin and temptation, think of yourself as a corpse. You are utterly dead and lifeless and incapable of responding and insensitive to every attempt by sin to get the consent of your will. Temptation walks up to you and says, "Hey, have I got a deal for you." But there is no response. You can't hear it speak. You can't watch it as it approaches. You can't smell it. You can't touch it. You can't think about it. You can't taste it. Why? Because you're dead to it. You have no capacity to respond to it.

Now, that's the ideal. Unfortunately, we are all too much alive to sin and temptation. But the aim of our growth as Christian men and women is to become increasingly insensitive to sin and temptation, to become increasingly unresponsive to it. We'll never be totally dead to sin until we are fully alive in heaven. But that's the goal toward which we are striving. Once again, Peter's point here is that Christ died for you and bore the punishment you deserved and endured God's wrath for sin precisely so that you might find the strength and motivation and incentive for saying no to sin in your daily life and yes to righteousness and purity and godliness.

We've seen him say this twice already, and now in verses 24b–25 he says it a third time: "By his wounds you have been healed. For you were straying like sheep, but have now returned to the Shepherd and Overseer of your souls." Peter is very clearly alluding to Isaiah 53:4–5, where the prophet declared,

Surely he has borne our griefs
    and carried our sorrows;
yet we esteemed him stricken,
    smitten by God, and afflicted.
But he was pierced for our transgressions;
    he was crushed for our iniquities;
upon him was the chastisement that brought us peace,
    and with his wounds we are healed.

And the most glorious news of all this is that by suffering for us and by bearing our sins in his body and by enduring our wounds or stripes, God has made it possible for us to return to the "Shepherd and Overseer" of our souls (v. 25b)!

I've written at length about what it means to say that God has laid on Jesus your sins because everything else that God has done with your sin is true because—indeed, *only* because—he has first exacted from Christ the penalty that your sins and mine so justly deserved.

Paul's Perspective

I briefly alluded to Paul's comments on 2 Corinthians 5 above. Let's now look more closely at what he says so we may gain an even greater understanding of what God did with our sin when he laid it on his Son.

> All this is from God, who through Christ reconciled us to himself and gave us the ministry of reconciliation; that is, in Christ God was reconciling the world to himself, not counting their trespasses against them, and entrusting to us the message of reconciliation. Therefore, we are ambassadors for Christ, God making his appeal through us. We implore you on behalf of Christ, be reconciled to God. For our sake he made him to be sin who knew no sin, so that in him we might become the righteousness of God. (2 Cor. 5:18–21)

This is a rich and wide-ranging treasure house of theological truth. But the more I think about it, the more I'm convinced that the brief comments of Scottish theologian James Denney (1856–1917) will suffice. I strongly suspect you'll agree after reading them. So, I ask that you do more than merely read his words (please, for your own sake, don't skip over them). Meditate on the profound implications of what he says. I'll interject a few relevant comments along the way.

Denney begins with a question, the answer to which is foundational to understanding the core of Christianity:

> What is it that makes a Gospel necessary? What is it that the wisdom and love of God undertake to deal with, and do deal with, in that marvelous way which constitutes the Gospel? Is it man's distrust of God? Is it man's dislike, fear, antipathy, spiritual alienation? Not if we accept the Apostle's teaching. The serious thing which makes the Gospel necessary, and the putting away of which constitutes the Gospel, is God's condemnation of the world and its sin; it is God's wrath, "revealed from heaven against all ungodliness and unrighteousness of men" (Rom. 1:16–18). The putting away of this is 'reconciliation'; the preaching of *this* reconciliation is the preaching of the Gospel.[11]

Here Denney touches on something rarely considered by most Christians. Let me put it in slightly different terms. From what is it that we need to be saved? Certainly not "from ourselves" (although one often hears such language, even in the church). Most Christians would say from hell. In a sense, they are correct. But why is hell a threat, and what is it that accounts for the existence of hell and the experience of those who end up there?

The answer, as Denney points out, is divine wrath. Our only hope is for God to save us from himself! This is the great glory of the gospel, that God in his grace takes action in Christ to save us from God in his wrath. God is not pitted against himself in this marvelous act of mercy, for God honors God when his love makes provision to satisfy the demands of his wrath.

11 James Denney, *The Second Epistle to the Corinthians* (London: Hodder and Stoughton, 1894), 212.

As stated earlier in chapter 2, divine justice and its expression in divine wrath against sin, to use Paul's words, call for the reckoning or "counting" of our trespasses "against" us (2 Cor. 5:19). So how is it that, instead, I am forgiven the guilt of these wicked deeds? The answer of the apostle, in verse 21, is that God "made him [Jesus] to be sin who knew no sin, so that in him we might become the righteousness of God." Don't ever think that the love of God means that the wrath of God was ignored. Because God is just and righteous, there must be a reckoning or "counting" of trespasses. But because God is loving and gracious, the "counting" or "imputing," and the punishment it entailed, fell on Christ.

I've often said to people that the reason the psalmist declares that God "does not deal with us according to our sins" (Ps. 103:10, a text we'll look at later) is that God dealt with Jesus according to our sins! Grace and mercy do not mean that sin is not dealt with, as if to suggest that God merely swept our sins under the carpet of his compassion and ignored the horrid offense of our rebellion. Far from it! God the Father "counted" our trespasses against God the Son and in doing so brought about the reconciliation.

Again, this "counting" or "reckoning" of our sins against him is what he means in 2 Cor. 5:21 when he speaks of Jesus being "made to be sin" on our behalf. Paul is talking about the liability to suffer the penal consequences of the law. Our guilt, incurred because of our trespasses, has been imputed to him so that we, through faith in his sufferings on our behalf, might have his righteousness imputed to us!

We must not overlook the fact that all this was achieved by him who "knew no sin." That as God he is without sin goes without saying, "but what is of vital importance for us and our reconciliation is that as Man, that is, in His incarnate state, Christ knew no sin, for only on that ground was He qualified to effect an atonement as Man for man."[12]

Now back to Denney:

> When St. Paul says that God has given him the ministry of reconciliation, he means that he is a preacher of this peace. He ministers reconciliation to the world. . . . It is not the main part of his vocation to tell men to make their peace with God, but to tell them that God has made peace with the world. At bottom, the Gospel is not good advice, but good news. All the good advice it gives is summed up in this—Receive the good news. But if the good news be taken away; if we cannot say, God has made peace, God has dealt seriously with His condemnation of sin, so that it no longer stands in the way of your return to Him; if we cannot say, Here *is* the reconciliation, receive it,—then for man's actual state we have no Gospel at all.
>
> When Christ's work was done, the reconciliation of the world was accomplished. When men were called to receive it, they were called to a relation to God, not in which they would no more be against Him—though that is included—but in which they would no more have Him against them. There would be no condemnation thenceforth to those who were in Christ Jesus."[13]

Becoming the "righteousness of God" (v. 21) is not simply a tall order but an impossible one. Yet there he says it: in Christ Jesus we have "become the righteousness of God"! As inconceivable as it may seem, notes Thomas Hooker, from a human point of view,

---

12 Philip E. Hughes, *Paul's Second Epistle to the Corinthians* (Grand Rapids, MI: Eerdmans, 1973), 212.

13 Denney, *Second Epistle to the Corinthians*, 213–15.

"such we are in the sight of God the Father as is the very Son of God himself. Let it be counted folly or frenzy or fury or whatever. It is our wisdom and our comfort; we care for no knowledge in the world but this: *that man hath sinned and God hath suffered; that God hath made himself the sin of men, and that men are made the righteousness of God.*"

The foundational truth of penal substitution is so critical that I've devoted a lengthy chapter to unpacking what it means. So, pause, ponder this truth, and give God praise for what he has done with your sin by laying it on his Son. We're now ready to dive into the other eleven things God has done with your sin, as well as the three things he'll never do.

3

He Has Forgiven You of Your Sins

"It's just a word. It doesn't mean a thing."

"Which word is that?"

"*Forgiveness.* I've heard it a thousand times. But you can't just say it or believe it and make the past disappear. Guilt is forever. There's nothing anyone can do about it."

"Does that include God?"

"Especially God. He never forgets. He carries all his grudges forever."

Such was the flow of my conversation with a young man who had become addicted to pornography and filled his days with all manner of sexual fantasies and lust. I wouldn't want you to think that his beliefs about the possibility, or impossibility, of forgiveness were spoken without passion or regret. Tears flowed. At one point, I thought he would hyperventilate and pass out. But he regained his composure.

"What if it were possible for you to be completely and eternally forgiven? What if you could know with absolute certainty that all your sins could be wiped clean and the guilt and the feelings of rejection could be banished from your heart?"

"You're preaching again, Sam. Cut it out. I need to hear truth."

"I'm preaching truth. Unassailable truth. Truth you can count on."

"But how? Where does my sin go? Does God just push delete on my guilt and it suddenly vanishes from sight? Or does he wave some magic wand of mercy over my head or sprinkle pixie dust and say, 'Abracadabra'?"

"No. He took your sin and the punishment you should have suffered and placed it on Jesus. Jesus took it willingly. He took it because he loves you. Whatever debt you owed, he paid. Whatever justice you deserved, he endured it. Whatever wrath should have fallen on you, fell on him. Can you believe that?"

"I don't know. It sounds a bit too good to be true."

"It's better than 'good.' It's great! It's glorious! It's the good news of the gospel."

After considerable dialogue and a reflection on a whole list of biblical texts that speak of forgiveness, Jimmy broke down in tears and cried out in faith for Jesus to save him and forgive him his sins.

I'm sure King David processed his need for forgiveness differently from how Jimmy did. But the result was the same. David had committed adultery. He had stolen from another man. He had defiled a woman who wasn't his wife. He had defiled himself. He schemed to have her husband killed. But worst of all, he had violated the honor, glory, and goodness of his God. Is forgiveness still possible for someone like that? Someone like Jimmy? Someone like you?

The point of this book is to do everything I can to convince you that the answer is yes. We saw in the previous chapter the foundational truth that makes everything else possible. God the Father took the guilt and well-deserved condemnation that was rightfully ours and "laid" it on Jesus (Isa. 53:6). Jesus, in love and from a desire to make known his glory and grace to countless hell-deserving sinners like Jimmy and David and you and me, yielded himself up on the cross. And the result? Was it all in vain? Did anything good come of it? Oh my, yes! It's called forgiveness.[1]

I often think we have misunderstood what David meant when, upon receiving forgiveness for his multiple transgressions, he cried out, "Blessed is the one whose transgression is forgiven, . . . / Blessed is the man against whom the Lord counts no iniquity" (Ps. 32:1, 2). What did he mean by the word "blessed"? I think David meant something more than simply that he was in good standing with God, now that the guilt of his sin had been removed. Surely he is describing for us his internal, heartfelt, feeling of being clean in the sight of God. There is indescribable joy, says David, that comes with being set free from the penalty of one's sins. There is an emotional delight, a sense of well-being, a deep and abiding joy that is bound up with the reality of forgiveness. And it is something so profoundly liberating that David can't help but encourage others to lay hold of this glorious reality:

Therefore let everyone who is godly
	offer prayer to you at a time when you may be found;

---

1 Much in this chapter appeared earlier in two of my books: *The Singing God: Feel the Passion God Has for You . . . Just the Way You Are* (Lake Mary: Passio, 2013), 59–70; and *More Precious Than Gold: 50 Daily Meditations on the Psalms* (Wheaton, IL: Crossway, 2009), 92–96.

surely in the rush of great waters,
    they shall not reach him.
You are a hiding place for me;
    you preserve me from trouble;
    you surround me with shouts of deliverance. (Ps. 32:6–7)

When the flood waters of adversity and opposition begin to rise, seek the higher ground that only God can provide. When enemies threaten you with trouble, God is the perfect hiding place, a shelter in whom we find safety and protection from all that assaults the soul. And remember, this is precisely for men and women like David and Jimmy who have spurned God's ways and transgressed his will.

Why would God do this for someone like David or Jimmy or for you and me? What accounts for this willingness in God to forgive? To what do we attribute the peace and release and joy that flood the pardoned soul? David puts his finger on it in Psalm 32:10: "Many are the sorrows of the wicked, / but steadfast love surrounds the one who trusts in the Lord." God's love is the bulwark of our lives, the bodyguard of our souls, the atmosphere of immutable affection in which we move and live and breathe. Perhaps you are still like Jimmy, asking, "Is forgiveness really possible?" It may sound like a silly question, especially to a Christian audience that I assume knows what the Bible says about God's grace and redemption and the forgiveness of sin through faith in Christ. But even for Christians, sometimes "forgiveness" is only a word lost in a stack of abstract theological language that we speak and confess and recite and even affirm in the liturgy. But if you're anything like me, none of this matters if I can't receive forgiveness into the depths of my soul and experience its liberating, life-changing power and taste its sweetness.

So, let me ask again: Is forgiveness possible? Can a thief be forgiven? What about an adulterer? What about a woman who's had an abortion, or a man who's paid for one? What about Jimmy? What about those failures, those sins, committed long ago, forgotten by everyone else but still lingering in our spiritual memory, sins whose guilt and shame we carry around tucked away safely in our hearts? Is forgiveness possible?

Why is it so important for us to answer that question? It's important because of something I once heard John Piper say. The only sin that can be defeated, said Piper, is a sin that has been forgiven. There are countless natural ways to overcome bad habits and repeated failures: therapies, formulas, willpower, and more. But they all produce only self-righteousness, not the righteousness of God. Piper's point is that being right with God must precede doing right for God. That's why our question is so crucial.

Let's go back to David for a moment. For a season in time, he kept quiet about his sin. He suppressed it. He shoved it deep down inside, thinking it gone for good. He ignored the tug on his heart. He denied the pain in his conscience. He numbed his soul to the persistent pangs of conviction. We often do the same thing. We turn to food, alcohol, sex, TV, the internet, shopping, or whatever form of spiritual anesthetic we find helpful. Anything is better than wrestling with the agony of a defiled conscience.

Then one day, the prophet Nathan told David a story. It was all about a rich man who stole the one little ewe lamb of a poor man rather than taking a sheep from his own huge flock. "Surely this man deserves to die," shouted an enraged David.

With a bony finger pointed at David's nose, Nathan calmly declared, "You are the man! . . . Why have you despised the word of the LORD, to do what is evil in his sight? You have struck down Uriah the Hittite with the sword and have taken his wife to be your wife" (2 Sam. 12:7, 9).

Adultery and murder make for a sensational story. Many a TV miniseries have rocketed to the top of the Nielsen ratings on the wings of those two sins. Rarely, though, does Hollywood portray the anguish and turmoil they inflict. Listen to what David confesses in Psalm 32 about the impact of his sin as it festered unconfessed and unforgiven in his heart. Then listen more closely still to the song of God's forgiving love:

> For when I kept silent, my bones wasted away
>   through my groaning all day long.
> For day and night your hand was heavy upon me;
>   my strength was dried up as by the heat of summer.
>   (vv. 3–4)

Someone described David's anguish as "the inner misery of the lacerated heart." David "kept silent" about his sin. He ignored the voice of the Holy Spirit and suppressed the piercing conviction that stabbed repeatedly at his conscience. He refused to deal openly and honestly and forthrightly with God. He would not face his sin. He was living under the delusion that if he could somehow forget about it, God would too.

David portrays the impact of his sin in physical terms. Some think this is metaphorical language, that David is using physical symptoms to describe his spiritual anguish. Whereas that's possible, I suspect that David was feeling the brunt of his sin in his body as well. What we see here is a law of life in God's world. If you bottle up sin in your soul, it will eventually leak out like acid and eat away at your bones. Unconfessed sin is like a festering sore. You can ignore it for a while, but not forever.

The physical effects of his spiritual choices are agonizingly explicit. There was dissipation: "my bones wasted away" (cf. Ps. 6:2). There was distress: "my groaning all day long." And David was drained: "my strength was dried up as by the heat of summer." Like a plant withering under the torrid desert sun, so too was David dried up and drained from suppressing his sin.

In other words, he was quite literally sick because of his refusal to come clean with God. His body ached because his soul was in rebellion. Spiritual decisions always have physical consequences. "The Spanish Inquisition," wrote Charles Spurgeon, "with all its tortures was nothing to the inquest which conscience holds within the heart."[2]

God loves his children too much to let them sin with impunity. It was in fact God's hand that lay heavily on David's heart. To sin without feeling the sting of God's disciplinary hand is the sign of illegitimacy. Our instinctive reaction to the distress and turmoil that come in the wake of sin is to conclude that God hates us and has now abandoned us for good. But David knew what his own son Solomon would later declare: "My son, do not despise the LORD's discipline / or be weary of his reproof, / for the LORD reproves him whom he loves, / as a father the son in whom he delights" (Prov. 3:11–12; cf. Heb. 12:5–11).

All of us can identify with David's reluctance. No one likes to admit being wrong. No one relishes the thought of confession, far less something as serious as adultery and murder. Facing our faults, whether intellectual or moral, is terribly discomforting.

2 Charles H. Spurgeon, *Treasury of David*, vol. 1 (Peabody, MA: Hendrickson Publishers, n.d.), part 2:82.

But here is the good news: This psalm is not primarily about the agony of denial and the pain of repression. It is about the joy and blessedness of forgiving love! Listen again to David's joyful cry:

> Blessed is the one whose transgression is forgiven,
>> whose sin is covered.
> Blessed is the man against whom the LORD counts no iniquity,
>> And in whose spirit there is no deceit. . . .
>
> I acknowledged my sin to you,
>> and I did not cover my iniquity;
> I said, "I will confess my transgressions to the LORD,"
>> and you forgave the iniquity of my sin. (Ps. 32:1–2, 5)

David ransacks the dictionary to describe the full extent of his failure. He calls what he did a "transgression" (v. 1), a word that refers to the rebellious and disloyal nature of his actions. He refers to it as a "sin" (v. 1), a word that points to any act that misses the mark of God's revealed will. And he calls it "iniquity" (v. 5), that is to say, a crooked deed, a conscious intent to deviate from what is right.

Why do you think David goes to such verbal lengths to portray his sin? My sense is that he does so to emphasize that every sin, any sin, whatever its cause or character, no matter how small or big, secret or public, intentional or inadvertent, can be forgiven!

David also uses three different words to describe his confession (v. 5). He "acknowledged" his sin to the Lord. He refused to "cover" his iniquity. He was determined to "confess" his transgressions. Nothing is held back. There is no cutting of corners. No compromise. He comes totally clean. All the cupboards of his soul are emptied. All little black books are opened and read aloud. His confession is like opening the floodgates of a dam. It may be messy at first, but the release of ever-increasing pressure is life to his burdened heart.

Three different words for sin. Three different words for confession. But better still, three different words for forgiveness!

Blessed is the man whose transgressions are "forgiven" (v. 1). The word literally means "to carry away." David's sin, my sin, your sin, is like an oppressive weight from which we long to be relieved. Forgiveness lifts the burden from our shoulders.

Blessed is he whose sin is "covered" (v. 1). That's yet another thing God has done with our sin that we'll take up in a later chapter. Here I will simply point out that it's as if David says, "Oh, dear Father, what joy to know that if I will 'uncover' (v. 5) my sin and not hide it, you will!" David doesn't mean to suggest that his sin is merely concealed from view but somehow still present to condemn and defeat him. The point is that God sees it no more. He has covered it from all view.

Blessed is that man or woman, young or old, whose sin the Lord does not impute or count against them (v. 2). No record is kept. God isn't a spiritual scorekeeper to those who seek his pardoning favor! I don't know how all this affects you, but I agree with David when he says (shouts?), "Blessed is the one whose transgression is forgiven, . . . / *Blessed* is the man against whom the LORD counts no iniquity" (vv. 1–2).

What, Then, Is Forgiveness?

What does it mean for God to "forgive" our sin? It means that he promises never to hold our sin against us in order to justify our rejection or judgment. In other words, when forgiveness has occurred, *there no longer exists any legal or moral grounds on the basis of which God might condemn you or me.* The punishment that sin requires is no longer a threat because it has been laid upon someone else—our substitute, Jesus Christ.

But to be forgiven also means that God promises never to bring up our sin or to remind us of it or to use it in any way to manipulate us or threaten us or to justify some action he may be taking in relationship with us. In other words, to have our sins forgiven means that they simply no longer register or appear on God's radar! They no longer factor in any relevant or meaningful way into the eternal relationship we have with him.

Earlier, I made a distinction between our eternal union with God and our experiential communion with him. When our sins are forgiven, no sin—past, present, or future—can disrupt or sever our union with our heavenly Father. But we must reckon with the fact that when we sin and fail to repent and confess, our experiential communion with God can be sorely shaken. Our capacity to see his beauty and enjoy his majestic mercy is clouded and dulled. But this can be quickly overcome by heartfelt acknowledgment of the ways we have defied and dishonored him.

A synonym of "forgive" is "pardon," as when God is said to "abundantly pardon" our transgressions (Isa. 55:7). The word "pardon" points us once again to the fact that God has declared that we are now and forevermore free from the condemning power of sin. We no longer need fear the punishment that comes with sin. We need no longer or ever again suffer the consequences of our transgressions, because Christ has suffered them in our place.

When the president issues a pardon to a condemned criminal, the criminal is immediately released from prison with the absolute assurance and guarantee that he will never endure another day of judgment or condemnation. His name is cleared. His reputation is restored. His standing in the sight of the court is now as one who is innocent. And such we are with God!

That's what God has done with your sin when you abandon all efforts at self-salvation and entrust your soul to Jesus Christ and the sufficiency of his penal substitutionary death in your place, and confidently look to his resurrection as your hope for eternal life.

And Jimmy? He's living in the joy of being forever and finally forgiven, and is daily experiencing the power to abandon his sinful ways and rest in the goodness of God's grace and kindness in Jesus.

There is a sense in which everything else that follows in this book is an unpacking of what it means to be forgiven. The many metaphors and analogies that the biblical authors employ are designed to drive home to our hearts, as vividly as possible, the breathtaking truth that God has dealt decisively in and through Jesus Christ to remove from us any and all grounds for condemnation.

Before leaving this subject, I want to give you one concrete and vivid illustration of what forgiveness is and how it liberates the soul from the burden of sin.

The "Look" of Love[3]

All of us are familiar with the story of how Peter denied Jesus three times. It is painful to read and, for some, even more difficult to understand how he could have done it. But there is something that transpired between Jesus and Peter that few Christians know. The reason is that it is mentioned only once, in Luke's gospel. There we are told that at the precise moment of Peter's third denial,

---

3   The following material first appeared in my book *To Love Mercy: Becoming a Person of Compassion, Acceptance, and Forgiveness* (Colorado Springs, CO: Navpress, 1991), 163–65.

just as the rooster crowed, "the Lord turned and looked at Peter" (Luke 22:61).

Pause for a moment and consider the majesty of divine providence. Consider how the Father orchestrated this moment with such precision and beauty. There must have been dozens of people everywhere, running back and forth, caught up in the frenzy of the events of that night. Yet in this moment, Jesus saw only Peter, and Peter saw only Jesus. Jesus is being shuttled back and forth, dragged through courtyards, in and out of rooms. Peter's loud cursing still echoed in the courtyard of Caiaphas, yet at precisely the moment the rooster crowed, Jesus turned and locked eyes with Peter. "And Peter remembered the saying of the Lord, how he had said to him, 'Before the rooster crows today, you will deny me three times.' And he went out and wept bitterly" (vv. 61–62).

When Jesus turned and looked at Peter, he saw an angry and defiant man, a man whose adamant declarations of undying allegiance had withered at the sound of a servant girl's voice. But what did Peter see when he looked at Jesus? Into what kind of eyes did he gaze? On what kind of face did he look? Was it the face of a well-groomed politician? Was it the face of a freshly washed, clean-shaven businessman? Hardly. He looked into blackened eyes, virtually closed from the savage beating Jesus had endured. Bruised cheeks, swollen jaw, bloodied nose, with the vile and venomous spittle of his mockers dripping from his beard.

Peter looked with horror at the face of Jesus, barely recognizable. With what sort of look did Jesus gaze back at Peter? There are all sorts of "looks." Our eyes alone can communicate virtually every human emotion:

There is the flirtatious look that passes between two teens in the hallway at school.

There is the intimidating stare of two boxers in the middle of the ring.

There are the "looks that kill," the looks that pass between two people after one has abandoned and betrayed the other.

There is the "I told you so" look, that unmistakable facial contortion reminding one of past failures and broken promises. It is a condescending glare, a look of smug superiority.

The look of anger is one we all know well. No words are necessary, only a disdainful sneer that says, "Some friend you turned out to be! Where were you when I needed you most?"

We've all been on the receiving (and sending) end of the look of resentment. I'm talking about one of those "after all I've done for you, this is what I get in return" looks.

Perhaps the most painful look of all is the one of disappointment. Combined with a sad shaking of the head it says, "You sorry, no-good bum. I should have expected something like this from someone like you."

But how did Jesus look at Peter? Perhaps at this point each of us needs to ask ourselves, "How does Jesus look at me when I fail him, deny him, turn my back on him?" Did Jesus peer into Peter's eyes with disdain or disappointment or anger or resentment? I don't think so. I wasn't there. I can only speculate. Neither Matthew nor Mark nor Luke nor John tells us. But knowing Jesus as I do, and seeing Peter's response, I think I have a pretty good idea.

I think Jesus turned toward Peter with a look that he recognized immediately, a look of incredible power, enough to bring down the stone barriers of a military fortress. In this case, it pierced the sinful walls of Peter's stricken heart. It was the same look Peter had seen so many times before: Zacchaeus, the woman at the well, the woman taken in adultery, so many lepers and prostitutes and tax collectors had been the focus of those penetrating eyes of love, hope, and forgiveness. And then Peter remembered, and he went outside and wept bitterly.

So what did Peter see in those bruised and bloodied eyes? There were no words uttered, but the eyes of Jesus spoke loudly and clearly:

It's okay, Peter. I know your heart. I know that deep down inside you really do love me. I know the brokenness and devastation you feel right now. It really is okay. I still love you as much now as I ever did before. I'm about to die for your threefold sin of denial. And you will be completely forgiven. It's okay."

It was more than Peter could believe. After what he'd done, knowing what he deserved, the eyes of Jesus said, "There's still hope."

But the story doesn't stop there. Again, I'm only speculating, but I don't think this look of loving forgiveness was in itself enough to get Peter "over the hump" and "back in the game," so to speak. It helped. Peter's broken heart was led to life-giving repentance. But something more needed to occur. Peter was probably still filled with self-doubt and anxiety, feeling disqualified as an apostle. I can almost hear him say, "Even if I'm forgiven, I can't believe Jesus would ever want to see me again. Even if he did, I'm probably forever disqualified from ministry. Better for everyone that I just slip away into the shadows."

But Jesus wasn't yet done with Peter. We read in Mark 16:1–8 of the events on Sunday, after the Sabbath. Mary Magdalene, Mary the mother of James, and Salome brought spices so that they might anoint Jesus's body. When they arrived at the tomb, they were stunned to see the stone rolled away and an angel dressed in a white robe. His words to them:

"Do not be alarmed. You seek Jesus of Nazareth, who was crucified. He has risen; he is not here. See the place where they laid him. But go, tell his disciples *and Peter* that he is going before you to Galilee. There you will see him, just as he told you." (vv. 6–7)

I can imagine that the risen Christ gave explicit instructions to that angel: "Now listen carefully. When you tell the women to report back to the disciples that I'll meet them in Galilee, be absolutely certain you mention Peter by name. Single him out. Make a point of him so those women will know without a doubt that he is included."

I wish I had been present to see the women rush into the room where the disciples had gathered. Out of breath, overcome by joy and indescribable excitement, they speak the words that none of the disciples ever expected to hear: "He has risen! The angel said to go to Galilee and Jesus would meet all of you there." At this point, I can almost imagine Peter, sitting in the corner, hiding in the shadows, hoping no one will notice his presence, saying to himself, "Well, that's great. He's alive. I'm happy for him. But there's no way I'm going to Galilee. I can't bear the thought of looking into his face again. Worse still, he probably can't bear the thought of looking at me."

"Oh, yeah. Peter," shouted Mary and Salome, "he mentioned you specifically. I'm not sure why, but that angel made a point of using your name. He singled you out. You're included. You're supposed to come, too. Jesus wants to see you."

Unless I miss my guess, that was when forgiveness became more than just a word for Peter. The reality of restoration and hope and cleansing and a fresh start came flooding into his soul, wave upon wave of joy and gratitude and delight. I suspect that many of you, maybe even most, believe that you have so horribly failed in your Christian life that you tremble at the thought of looking Jesus in the eye. It may not be as bad as Peter's denial of him. For some of you, it may be something even worse. But here is the only thing that matters: He still loves you. He's still for you. He's still here with you and has promised never, ever to leave you nor forsake you.

Perhaps you live in fear of the second coming of Jesus. Perhaps the prospect of looking at him, or even more so, the prospect of him looking at you, is terrifying. I can assure you of this: because of who he is, because of his unchanging character, because of the unbreakable promises he has made to you, because of his atoning death in your place and his bodily resurrection, when he looks you in the face, you will see the look of love and forgiveness and grace and kindness. I'm absolutely certain that you will see what Peter saw: a look of undying, never-ending, heartfelt love and joy. Be encouraged, Christian friend!

4

He Has Cleansed You of Your Sin

I'M A HUGE FAN OF the cartoon strip *Peanuts*. I rarely let a day go by that I don't check for the latest installment of the classic work of Charles Schultz. In spite of the latter's death, newspapers continue to publish his work. I simply can't get enough of them. Charlie Brown never seems to win, at anything, be it flying a kite, kicking a football, or making friends with that adorable little red-headed girl of his dreams. Even when his baseball team appears finally to have emerged victorious, they have to forfeit because Rerun, Lucy's younger brother, had gambled a nickel on the game! Everyone knows Snoopy and Linus and Schroeder and Peppermint Patty. But one character often goes unnoticed: Pigpen. His name fits, as each time he appears, a visible cloud of dust and bugs engulfs him. He's always dirty, grimy, and very much in need of a bath.

Often, and in the experience of some people, all the time, they feel like this on the inside. It isn't that they carry a swirl of dirt surrounding them on the outside. They feel grimy and soiled and filthy on the inside. They may well find that soap and shampoo are effective in cleaning the body, but the soul, well, that's another matter.

So, do you "feel" dirty? Does your heart ache with the stain of sin? Does guilt darken your emotions and paralyze you in your relationship with God? It need not! For God has cleansed you of your sin! How so, you ask? As we've seen, it all began when he laid your sin on Christ. This was the foundation for our being forgiven. And the forgiven soul is the clean soul, washed, rinsed, and made spiritually pure. I know how hard it is to believe this. Our experience on a daily basis mirrors that of those afflicted with leprosy during the lifetime of Jesus. They were required to warn in advance of their presence with the gut-wrenching scream, "Unclean! Unclean!" And that is how so many today feel. It isn't that they fear infecting others with some incurable disease. This affliction is of the heart and soul, not the body. But the inner turmoil is just as painful as the disfigured body. And thus to be told that God sees us clothed in the white righteousness of his Son is almost more than the finite human mind can comprehend.

Throughout Scripture, sin is portrayed as dark and ugly and dirty. It soils and spoils everything. It is like a deep, dark, seemingly indelible stain on our souls. It discolors and distorts everything. I sometimes laugh at the little things in life that remind me of this truth. Hanging in my closet is a white, long-sleeved shirt with a noticeable brown stain just above the front pocket. I've taken it to the cleaners on multiple occasions, making certain that they know how they failed to get it removed each time I've brought it in. And each time I pick it up, there is a piece of paper pinned to the shirt, right next to the stain, with the apology that nothing they've tried has been successful in cleaning the shirt of this visible blight. And they've tried everything! No detergent, rigorous scrubbing, spot remover, cleansing agent, soap, bleach, or disinfectant can remove it. Sometimes that's precisely how sin feels. Notwithstanding our best efforts and most sincere of intentions, we can't rid ourselves of its ugliness, like a deep-dyed ring around the collar.

Yet God appeals to us in Isaiah 1:18 with these wonderful words: "Come now, let us reason together, says the LORD: / though your sins are like scarlet, / they shall be as white as snow; / though they are red like crimson, / they shall become like wool."

When David finally came to grips with his adultery with Bathsheba and his complicity in the murder of her husband Uriah, he cried out to God, "Wash me thoroughly from my iniquity, / and cleanse me from my sin!" (Ps. 51:2). And in verse 7, "Purge me with hyssop, and I shall be clean; wash me, and I shall be whiter than snow." Never forget that this wasn't simply for David some 3,000 years ago. This is the promise of God to each believer today. It is for you, now and forevermore, if only you will lay hold of Christ by faith.

Psalm 51[1]

No one enjoys being exposed in public. Can you even imagine what it would feel like to have your sins announced from the platform in church on a Sunday morning? Or, worse still, looking on a screen or in a hymnbook and finding, much to your dismay, that your immorality or idolatry has been integrated into the lyrics of the worship song being sung. As hard as that is to imagine, that is what happened to David.

Psalm 51 is justifiably famous, but many overlook what is called the superscription. Scholars debate how much weight should be given to the subtitles you see above each psalm, but they are typically accurate portrayals of the historical context for what is found

---

1 Much in this chapter is adapted from my book *More Precious Than Gold: 50 Daily Meditations on the Psalms* (Wheaton, IL: Crossway, 2009), 138–47.

in the psalm. Have you ever paused to take notice of the superscription for Psalm 51? Each time I read it, I can almost hear David cry, "Ouch!"

To the choirmaster. A Psalm of David, when Nathan the prophet went to him, after he had gone in to Bathsheba.

You can almost hear the choir leader giving instructions to the audience: "Okay, folks, turn to number 132 in your hymn books and let's stand and sing all about how your leader had sex with a woman not his wife!"

You can read about David's sin in 2 Samuel 11:1–27, and how Nathan the prophet confronted him in 2 Samuel 12:1–15. The consequences of David's choices were monumental: (1) the death of the firstborn son of David and Bathsheba (2 Sam. 12:15–23); (2) trouble with Amnon, who raped Tamar, Absalom's sister (13:1–22); (3) the rebellion of Absalom (13:23–18:33); (4) trouble with affairs of state (e.g., the revolt of Sheba in 19:41–20:26). This is a healthy reminder that although David was fully and finally forgiven and had the dark stain of his sin wiped clean, there were devastating results that lingered long into his life.

David's heart is broken. His soul seems to feel as if it is splintered into a thousand pieces as he comes to grips with the fact that his sin is ultimately against God, and God alone (Ps. 51:4). That explains why the basis of his appeal for forgiveness isn't his military exploits on behalf of Israel or the lofty worship songs he wrote that comprise so much of the book of Psalms. David cries out to God for mercy. When we feel the sting of sin, our immediate reaction is to direct attention away from our failure and to some noteworthy accomplishment that we vainly imagine will atone for our missteps.

"Okay, Lord. Yes, I failed you yet again. But have you forgotten how generous I've been with my money? Do I have to remind you of the multiple sacrifices I've made and the inconveniences I've endured to help others in need?" As much as this may have been a temptation for David, he knows that his only hope is divine mercy.

Our primary concern is with one of the ways in which he beseeches God for forgiveness. He beseeches the Lord to "wash" him "thoroughly" from his iniquity (v. 2). Even more vivid is his appeal that God "purge" him "with hyssop." Then he will be "clean." "Wash me," he asks of the Lord, "and I shall be whiter than snow" (v. 7). This word translated "wash" was often used of a woman first saturating a garment with lye soap and then treading it under foot on a rock, beating and pummeling it as rushing waters poured over it. (I wonder whether that might work on my shirt?) One can almost hear David praying tearfully, "Gracious Lord, do that to my spirit! My sin is like a deep-dyed stain that has soiled the fabric of my soul, and no ordinary soap or detergent, far less any good works I might perform, can remove it. My transgressions are like ground-in dirt. Lord, scrub me clean by your mercy and grace!" Finally, the word "cleanse" was one used for ceremonial purification in the Old Testament.

Countless Christians know precisely what David is saying. They read his words and find themselves nodding with empathy. They feel spiritually paralyzed by the lingering stain of sin. Neither therapy nor religious formulas, neither good intentions nor good deeds, can erase the vivid memory of their transgressions or bring cleansing to the defiling sense of guilt. The oppressive weight of their failures is virtually suffocating.

That is why Psalm 51 is such a refreshing and heartwarming reminder of the hope of forgiveness. Let's look more closely at verse

7. David begins with an impassioned plea for ceremonial cleansing, cast in the form of what Hebrew scholars call synonymous parallelism: "Purge me with hyssop and I shall be clean; / wash me, and I shall be whiter than snow." David's choice of words is instructive. Hyssop, an aromatic herb with a straight stalk and a bushy head (it looked a lot like broccoli), was dipped in the blood of the sacrifice and then sprinkled seven times on the person who was defiled (see Lev. 14:1–9; Num. 19). The word translated "purge" might more literally be rendered "de-sin" me! Only then will David be "clean" and "whiter than snow." Can this actually happen for sinners like you and me?

Yes! But there is yet more. David lives in anticipation that he will "hear joy and gladness" and that his broken bones will once again "rejoice" (Ps. 51:8). This is a good reminder that the cleansing David desires is more than merely an objective standing with God. It is undoubtedly that, but being "clean" is also a subjective experience, an awakening in the heart of joy, gladness, and renewed hope. Then comes one of David's more famous requests, one with which all of us can identify:

> Create in me a clean heart, O God,
>   and renew a right spirit within me. (v. 10)

A "clean heart"? Really? Is this spiritual make-believe, or is this something that God extends to all who repent and trust in Christ alone? Yes, God really does this! You can have a clean heart today, before you ever finish reading this chapter. You don't have to read the other ten things God has done with your sin to know that your heart is clean, every stain of sin having been removed.

This image of being washed clean is found in numerous places in Scripture. I'll mention only a couple of them. In his letter to Titus, the apostle Paul describes what happens when a person is born again or regenerated by the Holy Spirit:

[God] saved us, not because of works done by us in righteousness, but according to his own mercy, by the washing of regeneration and renewal of the Holy Spirit, whom he poured out on us richly through Jesus Christ our Savior, so that being justified by his grace we might become heirs according to the hope of eternal life. (Titus 3:5–7)

The apostle John echoes this same truth, and in doing so refers to the cleansing agent by which this glorious miracle of spiritual washing occurs. No, it isn't by means of any of the products used by my neighborhood dry-cleaning business. According to John, "the blood of Jesus his Son cleanses us from all sin" (1 John 1:7). Yes, the strange irony is that a substance which typically creates an indelible stain—blood—in this case cleanses "us from all unrighteousness" (1 John 1:9). This is the marvelous and majestic truth of the saving, forgiving power of the shed blood of Christ Jesus.

Covid-19 and the Virus of Sin

I have no way of knowing the state of the world when this book is released, or when you may read it, but at the time of writing, the entire globe is still immersed in the Covid-19 pandemic that has so massively disrupted our daily routines. I can only hope that by the time you obtained this little book, the crisis is behind us. In any case, the understandable obsession with physical cleanliness is keeping pace with the spread of the virus itself.

Everywhere we look are signs demanding that we regularly wash our hands and refrain from touching our faces. Personal hygiene has become paramount. There is sitting on my desk a bottle of Purell that claims to kill 99.99 percent of all germs and bacteria. A rival product promotes the fact that it contains aloe vera and Vitamin E, and "leaves hands feeling soft." In the early stages of the pandemic, we heard of certain individuals who were hoarding a wide variety of hand cleansers and then selling them at exorbitant prices. At the office are numerous containers of disinfectant wipes that we are expected to apply generously to all surfaces and objects. The disinfectant claims to kill cold and flu viruses and virtually all bacteria within fifteen seconds.

Needless to say, the concern in the wake of Covid-19 is physical health. External cleanliness to guard us against infection is the goal. I don't want to be misunderstood, as if I'm suggesting that we shouldn't take steps to protect ourselves from such outbreaks of disease. I cite the current pandemic solely to highlight the immeasurably more important issue of spiritual cleanliness. The worst that Covid-19 can do to me is take my physical life. Any form of physical infection from a lethal virus can do only so much. But the virus contracted from spiritual rebellion and the eternal consequences it imposes on the destiny of men and women are far more severe.

It is staggering to think that so many people obsess over their physical welfare but give little to no thought to the state of their soul. Physical existence is a precious gift of God, to be guarded and preserved and used for the glory of God and the good of other people. But as James reminds us, we are "a mist that appears for a little time and then vanishes" (James 4:14). He isn't addressing the quality of life in this passage, as if his concern is to diminish the value of our earthly existence. He is talking about the quantity or duration of our lives, which is inescapably subject to the will of God (James 4:15).

When the Old Testament Levitical law speaks repeatedly of regulations concerning external or physical purity and the potential for defilement, the point is to direct us to the urgent need for spiritual and moral cleanliness in the sight of an infinitely pure and righteous God. There is no greater threat to the human heart than the virus of sin, that insidious infection that cannot be cured or wiped clean by any physical disinfectant. Only the blood of Jesus Christ, applied to the human heart by faith, can avail to deliver us from a death far worse than any physical demise.

David's fervent request is that God would "wash" him thoroughly from his "iniquity" and "cleanse" him from his "sin" (Ps. 51:2). And this is something that not all the handwashing in the world can accomplish. Everywhere I look today, I see people observing the call for social distancing. In a pandemic, keeping our physical distance from one another is essential. We lament not being able to shake hands and embrace one another and we long for the day when physical intimacy can be renewed. But the impact of our sin in having separated us from God is far more distressing. It is one thing to live each day at some distance from all others. It is something altogether different to be cut off from our Creator and consigned to eternal separation in which there is no intimacy, no contact, no communication of any sort (2 Thess. 1:9).

The good news of Scripture is that God in his great and unfathomable mercy has provided the ultimate cleansing agent, the shed blood of Jesus Christ, "like that of a lamb without blemish or spot" (1 Pet. 1:19). And that is what God has done with our sin.

The Joy of Feeling Clean

Some make far too much of our emotional life, while others do everything they can either to ignore or suppress the affections of the heart. But one thing is certain: "Our heavenly Father," says Packer, "intends his children to know his love for them, and their own security in his family."[2] This is more than mere cognitive acknowledgment that God loves us and has cleansed us from our sin. And it is far more profound than a fleeting emotion. It is what Packer calls "feeling knowledge."[3] This is what David was pleading for in Psalm 51. In asking that he might "hear joy and gladness" and that his bones might "rejoice" (v. 8), David is asking that God would grant him "feeling knowledge," the experiential awakening of the truth that he is genuinely clean in the sight of God.

Later in the psalm, he asks that God would "restore" to him "the joy of your salvation" (v. 12). Being cleansed from the stain of sin, saved and forgiven, is truly the most wonderful truth we could ever hope to hear and understand. But God wants us to enjoy, relish, and rest in what we know to be true. To this end, he gives us his Spirit, who quickens our hearts and floods us with "joy that is inexpressible and filled with glory" (1 Pet. 1:8). This is what the apostle Paul had in mind when he prayed that we might be "strengthened with power through his Spirit" in our inner being (Eph. 3:16). And why? So that we might be enabled "to comprehend with all the saints what is the breadth and length and height and depth, and to know the love of Christ that surpasses knowledge" (vv. 18–19). To this end, "God has sent the Spirit of his Son into our hearts, crying, 'Abba! Father!'" (Gal. 4:6).

2   J. I. Packer, *Knowing God* (Downers Grove, IL: IVP, 1993), 227.
3   Packer, *Knowing God*, 227.

May I then conclude this chapter by praying for you? Better still, turn this prayer into your own, as you ask the Father, through the Spirit, on the basis of the sin-bearing work of the Son on the cross, to awaken you in fresh and deeper ways to what it means to be cleansed from sin:

Most gracious and loving heavenly Father, I struggle for words to express my gratitude for the indescribable sacrifice you made in not sparing your Son but giving him for me as a penal substitutionary sacrifice. Lord Jesus, thank you for being willing to endure in my place the wrath and judgment I deserved, forever banishing the possibility that I would ever suffer the just deserts of my sins. Holy Spirit, please open my eyes and touch my affections so that I might more clearly see what the Father, through his Son, has done with my sin, and rejoice and celebrate and experience the peace that comes from the "felt knowledge" that I am now and forevermore clean. Amen.

5

He Has Covered Your Sin

EVERYONE, TO ONE DEGREE or another, fears exposure. There are some who live in constant fear of it and have cultivated relational styles that work well at keeping others at arms' length. A few intentionally work on developing a personality type that will guard their hearts and hide their faults. They are terrified that if someone were to see them as they know themselves to be, the result would be rejection or mockery.

The very notion of being vulnerable to others is paralyzing. Such people are so convinced that they will always fall short of the expectations of friends and family that they devote themselves to covering up every conceivable flaw. To be known and seen is to run the risk of being cast aside as unworthy. It takes a profound confidence in God's acceptance of oneself to peel back the layers of self-protection and let others in.

We see this in our world today in the countless efforts that are made to cover certain physical blemishes or flaws that we fear will cause people to laugh at us or turn away in disgust. Whether it's yet one more facelift or dose of Botox, or perhaps that awkwardly positioned and quite obvious toupee, we labor to hide from others what we fear will bring scorn should it be seen. But worse still is the apprehension that paralyzes us for fear that the weaknesses of my personality, the moral missteps of my past, or the low-grade daily addictions against which I struggle in the present will be made public.

But to know that God knows is more terrifying still. That is what makes the request of David in Psalm 139 so remarkable:

Search me, O God, and know my heart!
   Try me and know my thoughts!
And see if there be any grievous way in me,
   and lead me in the way everlasting! (vv. 23–24)

"No way," you say. "I don't want anyone, much less God, to search me and discover what I've labored so long to keep hidden." The potential for God to "know" our hearts drives many into utter emotional and relational seclusion. That God should be aware of the "thoughts" that race through our minds is unnerving. Of course, the irony here is that we don't have a choice! God does search us and know us, even if we don't want him to. This is what David acknowledged earlier in the psalm (vv. 1–4).

The worst thing of all about being known and seen is when it involves our sin. I'm happy for you to know that I hate squash and that I've never played a video game. That's no threat to my sense of psychological well-being. I don't mind much that you know about my foul temper, one that on more than one occasion got me banned from the local golf course. Now, mind you, I was in high school at the time, and this occurred fifty years ago! I'm sufficiently far removed from that episode that I can laugh about it now.

But press into my heart now, today, and ask me to share my inner struggles and the temptations to which I yield is another matter entirely. Most times when we're pressed by others, even if we know they have our best interests at heart, our inclination is to hide and to cover our sins and faults and shortcomings. We don't want others to see the real "me" but the "me" that I have created to make an impression and to avoid shame and ridicule.

And that is what brings us to yet another way that God has dealt with our sin. We find this truth in several texts. Here are two:

Blessed is the one whose transgression is forgiven,
whose sin is covered. (Ps. 32:1)

You forgave the iniquity of your people;
you covered all their sin. (85:2)

Again, why do you "cover" something? We cover our eyes lest we see something horrifying that we fear may haunt us in our dreams later that night. We cover up our tracks lest someone see that we were present in a place where we shouldn't have been. We cover a close personal friend by taking the blame for crimes or sins he or she has committed. We hear often that the entire story is a "cover-up" to protect the reputation or position of a politician. Adam and Eve covered up their nakedness, lest they be seen and experience the shame of exposure. At other times, it may be to keep something warm or to protect someone from danger.

But in the case of our sins, God covers them in order to *hide them from view*. Of course, in the most literal sense, our sins are often subject to public visibility. They may even get written on the internet or in the local newspaper. The promise that God will "cover" our sin does not mean he will make certain no one ever finds out about the things we have done. That would be impossible. In fact, we saw this in the case of King David in the previous chapter. The point, rather, is that our sins have been forever covered by God through the blood of Jesus Christ in the sense that they can no longer be used against us to bring condemnation or judgment.

So let's not press the imagery beyond what it can reasonably be understood to mean. As omniscient, God sees and knows everything. But the imagery of God covering our sin is intended to reassure our hearts that such sin will never be exposed for the purpose of being the legal grounds on which we might be cast aside or forsaken eternally.

Consider, by way of illustration, some brilliant prosecuting attorney who only recently "uncovered" new evidence that will lead to the conviction of the person on trial. We applaud such investigative excellence and are thankful that the threat such a person poses has been removed. But when it comes to the basis and security of our position in Christ, no amount of sinful evidence or proof of guilt will ever separate us from the love God has for us in Jesus.

Since we're on the subject of legal proceedings in a court of law, perhaps another illustration from an older TV program will help. Most people my age will remember *Perry Mason*, a Los Angeles criminal defense attorney played with considerable skill by Raymond Burr. The show was one of the more popular series on CBS and ran successfully for nine seasons. In all his cases, Mason was assisted by his private investigator, Paul Drake, and his secretary, Della Street.

Mason was a marvelous defense attorney. How marvelous? Well, in the entire course of the TV series, as best I can tell, he never lost a case. But that isn't altogether due to the fact that he possessed a sharp legal mind. It is also due to the fact that every client he defended was innocent! It stands to reason that with a good deal of digging and hard work, Mason's clients could count on him to secure an acquittal. The plot scheme was almost always the same. In the second half hour of each episode, either Mason or Drake would uncover previously unknown facts or evidence that exonerated Mason's client and implicated someone else.

There is an obvious and massive difference between Perry Mason and Jesus Christ. Unlike Mason, all Christ's clients are guilty! Jesus has never defended a single innocent person. And he makes no attempt to cover over the failures of those he represents. All the incriminating evidence is uncovered, exposed, and fully known. Notwithstanding the "guilty as charged" verdict that is rendered against us by the jury, we suffer no penalty. Those twelve men and women (hypothetically, of course), see everything. Their unanimous decision is always true. But in our case, the Judge has taken steps to cover our guilt! The knowledge of our crimes (sins) may spread far and wide. The newspapers may carry the story with all the gory and unpleasant details. But when it comes to the efforts of anyone to make use of those sins to condemn us, the Heavenly Judge overrules. He has taken steps through the voluntary sacrifice of our defense attorney, Jesus Christ, to fully satisfy the demands of the law. Whatever punitive consequences there may be for our spiritual felonies, Jesus has suffered them in our stead.

That is why God is fully just and righteous in taking steps to cover our sins. No law has been broken. No loophole has been exploited. Justice has been served, but in the person of our substitute. Now, I'm quite sure that the analogy breaks down in various ways, but the primary point remains. God will allow no one to see our sin for the purpose of indicting us. This is the glorious truth that Paul describes in Romans 8:

> What then shall we say to these things? If God is for us, who can be against us? He who did not spare his own Son but gave him up for us all, how will he not also with him graciously give us all things? Who shall bring any charge against God's elect? It is God who justifies. Who is to condemn? Christ Jesus is the one who died—more than that, who was raised—who is at the right hand of God, who indeed is interceding for us. (vv. 31–34)

These stunning statements directly challenge one of the more debilitating fears in the human heart: being stranded and left to ourselves, being trampled upon and exploited and taken advantage of and left with nothing. We are afraid of being exposed. We are paralyzed by the prospect that God will make use of our sin to undermine our very existence. The bottom line is that we are not persuaded that God really did lay our sin on his Son in our place and now and forevermore will make certain that all such sin is covered. Our fear is fueled by unbelief, and my principal aim in this book is to awaken confident trust that God really has dealt fully and finally with your sin.

Perry Mason would eloquently defend his clients against all wrongdoing. God doesn't. He and we openly acknowledge our individual guilt. So how does God win his case on our behalf and banish the accuser? He does it with the profound declaration that "Christ Jesus is the one who died" (v. 34) for us! The penalty that those sins call for—whether they be past, present, or yet future—has already been paid in full! How can anyone condemn you when Christ has already been condemned in your place? What is left for you to suffer? What guilt or penalty remains that might damage your relationship with God? Should any accusation from Satan or another human being be brought against you in the court of heaven with a view to uncovering your guilt, Jesus pleads your case. "Your Honor," he says, "the guilt for that sin has been laid on me. I died for it. Your justice has been satisfied. That sin, and all others like it, is covered!"

Can you now see the basis or ground on which Paul declares, "It is God who justifies" (v. 33)? He is the one who declares that you are acceptable in his sight, and no objection raised by the most clever of prosecuting attorneys will overturn his verdict.

Who shall separate us from the love of Christ? Shall tribulation, or distress, or persecution, or famine, or nakedness, or danger, or sword? As it is written,

"For your sake we are being killed all the day long;
we are regarded as sheep to be slaughtered."

No, in all these things we are more than conquerors through him who loved us. For I am sure that neither death nor life, nor angels nor rulers, nor things present nor things to come, nor powers, nor height nor depth, nor anything else in all creation, will be able to separate us from the love of God in Christ Jesus our Lord. (vv. 35–39)

Here again, Paul addresses that gnawing fear in your soul that some day, in some way, your sin will be unearthed and used against you. Oh, but far be it from the gracious and merciful God who did not spare his own Son but delivered him up for you to reverse course and uncover your sin. No, by no means ever, will this happen!

6

He Has Cast All Your
Sin behind His Back

THE STORY OF HEZEKIAH is familiar to most students of the
Bible, but let me briefly bring us all up to speed. Hezekiah was
only twenty-five years old when he ascended the throne as king
over Judah. If he died in 687 BC, as most evangelical scholars
believe, the fifteen additional years granted to him by the Lord
would place the year of his sickness in 702 BC. But I'm getting
ahead of myself.

As stated in Isaiah 38:1a, "Hezekiah became sick and was at the
point of death." The prophet Isaiah came to him and said, "Thus
says the LORD: Set your house in order, for you shall die, you shall
not recover" (v. 1b). Isaiah's bedside manner could probably use
some help—but, then, he was a prophet, not a physician! Hezekiah "wept bitterly" (v. 3) and responded by pleading with God
to extend his life. Once again, through Isaiah, the Lord said, "I
have heard your prayer; I have seen your tears. Behold, I will add
fifteen years to your life" (v. 5). As a confirming sign that God

would truly do this, he said, "'Behold, I will make the shadow cast by the declining sun on the dial of Ahaz turn back ten steps.' So the sun turned back on the dial the ten steps by which it had declined" (v. 8).

It isn't my purpose here to account for this astounding miracle. Many would dismiss it out of hand or explain it away as hyperbole. Some scoff at the notion that God could do this. But I concur with Alec Motyer who insists that

> it would be as improper for us to be dogmatic about how this was done as to deny what is plainly stated. Scripture presents the Creator God as the sovereign master of his creation, and the believing mind accepts that he could at will add ten units of time to that day. . . . The barest requirement of the verse is that the shadow moved, involving a divine manipulation of light whereby the shadow retreated (and did it then resume its former position?). But either way, a miracle of God was wrought in confirmation of his word to the king.[1]

After his recovery from this near-fatal illness, Hezekiah proclaimed,

> Behold, it was for my welfare
>   that I had great bitterness;
> but in love you have delivered my life
>   from the pit of destruction,
> for you have cast all my sins
>   behind your back. (v. 17)

1 J. Alec Motyer, *The Prophecy of Isaiah: An Introduction and Commentary* (Downers Grove, IL: InterVarsity Press, 1993), 292.

I believe I am justified in taking this language used by Hezekiah and applying it to us today. The imagery is vivid. It is as if God takes all our sin in hand and then throws it behind him, never to see it again, never to be influenced by it again, never again to take it into consideration when he deals with us or hears our prayers. He doesn't cast it behind *our* backs but behind *his*. David said his sin was always "before" him (Ps. 51:3), but when he confessed and repented, God put it behind his back.

I assume everyone recognizes that this is anthropomorphic language. That is to say, it is a portrayal of God using human form and shape in order to more effectively communicate the idea at hand. God doesn't have a back! Later on, we'll take note of yet another anthropomorphic image when God is described as trampling our sins under foot. Likewise, the portrayal of God with a "face" that he turns away from our sin falls into the same category. But we must never permit the use of such anthropomorphic language to diminish the force of what is being said. Simply because these are figures of speech does not mean that they don't communicate genuine, authentic—dare I say, literal—truth.

So again, what is the truth that this imagery is designed to convey? We need only think of the many times we seek to hide something from someone by placing it behind our backs. There is one sense in which this picture is inapplicable to God. When my daughters were considerably younger, and now also in the case of my grandchildren, I would hide a gift or some other object behind my back, but with the intention of then bringing it back before their eyes. It was all designed to heighten their anticipation of receiving something special as well as to increase the element of surprise.

As I'm sure you can see, this is something God will never, ever do in the case of our sins. The whole point of the imagery of God putting our sins behind his back is to emphasize that he will *never* suddenly bring them back into play or surprise us with them. There's nothing remotely enjoyable about thinking that God would do that with our sin in the way we do it with a special gift for our children.

God places our sins behind his back permanently and irreversibly. They are kept there so that no one—least of all God—can make use of them to condemn us. Whoever may try to sneak a peek, as it were, to see what God is holding firmly in his hand and out of view, will be rebuffed. It's as if God says, "I do not hold these sins in my hand in order to make use of them against the person who committed them. Quite the opposite is true. I hold them not for future use as grounds for condemnation but in order that no one, not even I, might appeal to such transgressions as a basis for condemning or rejecting the sinner."

What, then, does God intend for us and others to see, if not our sins? The righteousness of Jesus Christ! God views us as we are in his Son, by faith. We are united to Christ Jesus in an unbreakable spiritual covenant such that his righteousness is now truly ours. This is no legal fiction, as some have charged. This isn't make-believe. This is as real as it gets. The Judge of the universe has truly taken the righteousness of Jesus and imputed or reckoned or transferred it to us who have believed. It is ours—genuinely, eternally, personally.

This is the only thing about us that God will allow himself to see. It is very much what Paul had in mind when he wrote this in his letter to the Philippians:

But whatever gain I had, I counted as loss for the sake of Christ. Indeed, I count everything as loss because of the surpassing worth of knowing Christ Jesus my Lord. For his sake I have suffered the loss of all things and count them as rubbish, in order that I may gain Christ and be found in him, not having a righteousness of my own that comes from the law, but that which comes through faith in Christ, the righteousness from God that depends on faith. (Phil. 3:7–9)

When God, to use Paul's language, finds us, he finds us clothed in the alien righteousness of Jesus Christ. The word *alien* does not refer to extraterrestrial beings but to the fact that this righteousness comes from another, a person outside of and different from ourselves—namely, it is the righteousness of Jesus Christ himself.

Love: The Motive

There is one more critically important point to make, and it concerns the motive for God taking this sort of action to place our sins behind his back. I could have easily said this about all twelve things that God has done with our sin. I trust that you have already discerned this to be the case, but Hezekiah made it explicitly clear. Here again are his words:

> Behold, it was for my welfare
>   that I had great bitterness;
> but *in love* you have delivered my life
>   from the pit of destruction,
> for you have cast all my sins
>   behind your back. (Isa. 38:17)

The energy that stirred the heart of God to do this for Hezekiah, and the energy that likewise accounts for God doing it for us, is love.

There are numerous other biblical texts that assert the same truth. One thinks immediately of Paul's words in Ephesians 2. There he describes God, "being rich in mercy, because of the great love with which he loved us," making us alive together with Christ and seating us with him in the heavenly places (vv. 4–5). We are all capable at times of showing mercy to those in need. But our mercy is all too often measured and calculated. God is "rich" in mercy! His mercy is abundant and overflowing and never comes piecemeal. This mercy is especially revealed in the nature and quality of the love of God toward hell-deserving sinners. It is, says Paul, because of "the *great love* with which he loved us" that we are born again and saved. It would have been enough had Paul merely referred to God's "love" as the driving force in his merciful rescue of us from the consequences of our sin. But the Spirit obviously wanted this point to be heard loudly by those who are the objects of such affection. He wanted this truth to reverberate and echo throughout our souls. God's love for you and me is GREAT! Huge! Magnanimous! Effusive! Overwhelming! Lavish! Endless! Extravagant! Really, really big!

Let's be clear about one more critically important truth, one that I fear many Christians overlook. God's love for us, as seen in his taking action to lay our sins on his Son and placing our sins behind his back, was always designed so that we might get him. Get him? Get who? Get God! The removal of our sins was never the ultimate in the purpose of God, but only one necessary means to a yet higher and greater goal. Putting our sins behind his back and blotting them out and trampling them underfoot and casting them into the depths of the sea was always for the purpose of removing every obstacle that stood between God and us. As Peter put it, "Christ also suffered once for sins, the righteous for the

94

unrighteous, that he might bring us to God" (1 Pet. 3:18). In other words, getting us to God was always the ultimate aim of God's saving work in and through Jesus Christ.

This is why John Piper rightly titled his book *God Is the Gospel*.[2] The way God's love for Hezekiah and you and me is manifested is by his taking steps to do everything necessary so that we might gain him, be found in him (Phil. 3:9), be with him (Rev. 21:3), and see his face (Rev. 22:4).

This is the love of God that God works at great sacrifice to himself to give us himself! Hezekiah saw it and rejoiced in it. Can you do so as well?

---

2   John Piper, *God Is the Gospel: Meditations on God's Love as the Gift of Himself* (Wheaton, IL: Crossway, 2005).

7

He Has Removed Your Sin as Far as the East Is from the West

I'M NOT A SCIENTIST. Oh, how I wish I were! I simply don't have the brain for it. But that doesn't mean I don't try to understand science. The one area of science that has long fascinated me is astronomy. The sheer magnitude of the universe has always captivated my attention and fueled my imagination. This fixation on the heavens and all they contain was stimulated greatly by the creation of the Hubble Telescope.[1]

What you are about to read is no abstraction that bears no influence on your life. It is far more than mere statistics that account for the size of the universe. I can say that with confidence because of what the psalmist wrote:

> He does not deal with us according to our sins,
>   nor repay us according to our iniquities.

1 Some of what follows has been adapted from my books *More Precious Than Gold: 50 Daily Meditations on the Psalms* (Wheaton, IL: Crossway, 2009, 190–93, and *One Thing: Developing a Passion for the Beauty of God* (Ross-shire: Christian Focus, 2004), 88–91.

For as high as the heavens are above the earth,
    so great is his steadfast love toward those who fear him;
as far as the east is from the west,
    so far does he remove our transgressions from us.
    (Ps. 103:10–12)

As you've seen from the subtitle of this book, our focus is on not only the dozen things God has done with our sin, but also three things he never will do. Two of them are mentioned here. God does not and never will deal with us according to our sins. God does not and never will repay us according to our iniquities. We'll address both of these wonderful truths later on. But here, I want us to focus on the removal of our transgressions from us as far as the east is the from west.

I would be remiss, however, if I didn't say something about the intervening sentence. David rejoices in the fact that God's steadfast love toward those who fear him can be measured only by the height of the heavens above the earth. David was not an astronomer. He had no grasp of the unimaginable magnitude of the height to which he refers. But we do today.

A good illustration to help us fathom the unfathomable is the light-year. A light-year is how far light travels in 1 calendar year. If you have a big calculator, you can figure it out for yourself. Multiply 186,000 times 60, and you have a *light-minute*. Multiply that figure by 60, and you have a *light-hour*. Multiply that figure by 24, and you have a *light-day*, and that by 365, and you have a *light-year*. So, if light moves at 186,000 miles per second, it can travel 6 trillion miles (6,000,000,000,000) in a 365-day period. That's the equivalent of about 12,000,000 round trips to the moon.

Let's assume we are speeding in our jet airplane at 500 miles per hour on a trip to the moon. If we traveled nonstop, 24 hours a day, it would take us just shy of 3 weeks to arrive at our destination. If we wanted to visit our sun, a mere 93 million miles from Earth, it would take us a bit more than 21 years to get there. And if we wanted to reach Pluto, the (dwarf) planet farthest away in our solar system, our nonstop trip would last slightly longer than 900 years! Of course, we'd all be dead by then, but I trust you get the point.

Now, try to get your mind around this: The Hubble Telescope has given us breathtaking pictures of a galaxy some 13 billion light-years from Earth. Yes, 13 *billion* light-years! Remember, a light-year is 6,000,000,000,000 (6 trillion) miles. That would put this galaxy at 78,000,000,000,000,000,000,000 miles from Earth! In case you were wondering, we count from million, to billion, to trillion, to quadrillion, to quintillion, to sextillion. So, this galaxy is 78 sextillion miles from earth.

I can barely handle driving for more than 3 or 4 hours at 65 miles per hour before I need to stop and do something, either eat at McDonald's or, well, you know. The thought of traveling at 500 miles per hour nonstop, literally 60 minutes of every hour, 24 hours in every day, 7 days in every week, 52 weeks in every year, with not a moment's pause or delay, for—are you prepared for this?—20,000,000,000,000,000 years. That's 20 quadrillion years! And that would get us just to the farthest point that our best telescopes have yet been able to detect. This would be the mere fringe of what lies beyond.

Pause for a moment and let this sink in. Are you beginning to get a feel for what it means to know that God's love for you, that love that took unimaginable steps to remove the guilt of your sin, is greater than the distance between the heavens and the earth? Take as much time as you need.

If there is a clear sky tonight, go outside and gaze into the expanse above. Pick a star, any star. It seems fairly close. Want to visit? Surely it couldn't take that long to get there. It almost seems you can extend your hand and touch it. Well, not quite. The nearest star to us is a system of three called Alpha Centauri. The closest of those is Proxima Centauri, a mere 4.3 light-years from Earth. If we were bored with Pluto and wanted to extend our journey, speeding along nonstop, 24 hours a day, 7 days a week, 52 weeks a year, we would land on the closest star to Earth in a mere 6 million years! That's 500 miles per hour for 6,000,000 years. Beginning to get the picture? It's a very small illustration of how high the heavens are above the earth.

Let's speed up our travel a bit. Suppose our airplane was fast enough to go from Earth to the sun in only 1 hour. That's traveling at 93 million miles per hour. Imagine what that would do to the radar gun of your local police department! Traveling nonstop at 93 million miles per hour, it would still take us over 78 years to reach 61 Cygni, a star in the constellation Cygnus (the Swan), roughly 10.9 light-years from Earth.

If you aren't satisfied with visiting a single star, perhaps you'd like to take a look at the next galaxy in our cosmic neighborhood. The Andromeda Galaxy is a giant spiral, almost a twin of our own Milky Way galaxy. Astronomers have determined that there's probably a black hole at its center 1 million times the mass of our sun.

Although Andromeda is closest to us it's still a staggering 2.5 million light-years away (a mere 15 quintillion miles, or 15 followed by 18 zeros). On dark nights in the fall, it's barely visible to the naked eye as a small misty patch of light. Some are frightened to hear that it's moving toward us at 75 miles per second. No need to panic or rush to build a bomb shelter. At that pace, given its distance from earth, it might reach our Milky Way in about 6 billion years! Some say it will take only 3 billion years, so perhaps you should begin working on that bomb shelter after all!

In case you're wondering—on the assumption that your brain is still able to calculate the seemingly incalculable—our trip to Andromeda would last a paltry 4.2 trillion years (that's 4,200,000,000,000 years).

Here's one more for you to ponder: Shrink the earth to the size of a grapefruit. Pause for a moment and let the scale sink in. On this basis, the moon would be a ping-pong ball about 12 feet away. The sun would be a sphere as big as a 4-story building a mile away. Pluto would be an invisible marble 37 miles away. Now, put our entire solar system into that grapefruit. The nearest star would be over half a mile away. The Milky Way would span 12,000 miles! Now reduce the entire Milky Way to a grapefruit! The nearest galaxy to us, Andromeda, would be at a distance of 10 feet. The Virgo cluster would be a football field away.

Those calculations are the best I can do to explain how high the heavens are from the earth, all in order to illustrate how "great" God's steadfast love is for you. Incalculable love. Immeasurable love. Indecipherable love.

King David's point is that the distance between Earth and this distant galaxy, a mere 78 sextillion miles, is a pathetically small comparison to the likelihood that you will ever be dealt with according to your sins or repaid for your iniquities! If you were ever inclined to pursue your transgressions so that you might place yourself beneath their condemning power, 78,000,000,000,000,000,000,000 miles is an infinitesimally small fraction of the distance you must travel to find them!

One of the reasons we struggle to enjoy all that God is for us in Jesus is that we live under the influence of a lie. The lie is that our lifetime of sins, which often feels incalculable, is very close at hand, nearer to us than we feared. But David's assurance is that God has removed our sins from us "as far as the east is from the west." By "remove," he means that God has taken steps to eliminate any possibility that our sins and acts of idolatry and immorality could ever be used against us to justify our condemnation. And just how far is the east from the west?

Once again, we should remember that David is not speaking as a scientist. He's not giving us precise mathematical or astronomical calculations. He's trying to describe, as best he can, the utter impossibility that the penal consequences of our sins will ever return upon us. I'm quite sure that the way I will now explain David's language would be challenged by modern astronomers. But bear with me.

If I were to venture due east from my home in Edmond, Oklahoma, unhindered, undeterred, and in an immovable and unbending straight line, I would soon pass through the states of Arkansas, Tennessee, and North Carolina, before crossing the Atlantic Ocean into parts unknown. If my wife were to do the same going west, we would never again lay eyes on each other. She would travel through northern New Mexico, Arizona, and southern California before passing above the Pacific Ocean. Neither of us would ever reach the end of our journey. Don't think of this as two individuals traversing our globe, as if one launched out going east and the other going west, only to encircle the globe and finally bump into each other halfway around the world. David wasn't thinking in those terms. His point is that God takes the guilt of our sins and propels them eastward, and takes you and me personally and sends us westward, each on a perfectly straight line. When and where will the two ever meet up? Never, of course. And those are the chances, if you will, the odds, that you and I will ever encounter our sins or their power to condemn.

I've often wondered why the Spirit of God stirred the hearts of the biblical authors to make use of such extravagant and mind-bending images and illustrations. But I now think I know why. We—or perhaps I should speak only for myself. I am a hardheaded, slow-witted doofus who lacks the capacity to believe anything so wonderful as this. Were God to have written in the psalm that he loves us and has taken our sin away, that would, of course, have been enough for some people to fathom. When certain folk hear of the love of God, their response is something along the lines of: "Well, of course he loves me! I'm a lovable person! There's nothing so surprising about all that."

But for most of us, knowing ourselves as we do, it takes more than a simple affirmation of divine love for sinners to awaken us to the sheer magnitude of what God has done for us. It takes a comparison of the height of God's love with the height of the heavens above to drive home the point. It takes asking me to conceive of the inconceivable distance between east and west to open my eyes to this truth. I do not easily acknowledge God's love for me. If I were put in his place, I would never love me! God knows this, and has thus taken these elaborate verbal steps and the use of seemingly outlandish illustrations to overcome my resistance to the reality of his love. I hope and pray that it is beginning to sink into your soul as well.

8

He Has Passed Over Your Sin

IF YOU HAVE COME THIS FAR in the book and not wondered aloud, "What kind of God are you that you would do such things with our sins, the many ways that we have dishonored you and defied your will," then do it now. Stop, and ask the question: "Who is a God like you, forgiving us our sins and passing over the countless ways we have transgressed your revealed will?" Indeed, what kind of God is this? It certainly isn't the sort of God that we would have created, had we the power to do so. It simply stretches credulity to the breaking point to think that a God of immeasurable holiness and utmost justice could pass over the willful, defiant sins of the very people for whom he has already done so much.

I suspect we struggle to make sense of this sort of God because we would act in a contrary manner if we were in his place. Our response would be to get even, to exact an eye for an eye, to crush and destroy those who were so indescribably ungrateful and presumptuous. But we are not God. Thank God! He is. And he is of an altogether different nature from us.

This isn't to say that God doesn't bring judgment on those who refuse to repent, on those who exploit the weak for personal gain, on those who bow down before idols they have made with their own hands. The Old Testament book of Micah reveals to us yet again that God does not turn a blind eye from sin and apostasy. The book describes in chilling detail the judgments that come against the covenant nation for all its rebellious and idolatrous ways.

I have to be honest and say that reading the first six and a half chapters of Micah is frightening. Micah lived and prophesied toward the end of the eighth century BC, which would make him a contemporary of other Old Testament prophets such as Isaiah and Hosea. There was widespread corruption in both the northern kingdom of Israel and the southern kingdom of Judah. The prophets were not ministering words of truth and encouragement but were leading God's "people astray" (Mic. 3:5). God threatens them with a cessation of revelation. He will put "nothing into their mouths" (v. 5). There shall be no visions from heaven, as "the sun shall go down on the prophets, and the day shall be black over them" (v. 6). There is "no answer from God" (v. 7). He has gone silent.

Is there no hope? Has God forsaken his people forever? What has become of his promises to the patriarchs? Will he simply cast them aside and be done with them eternally? No! It does not come until the final verse of the book, but there we read that the God who judges is the same God who "will show faithfulness to Jacob and steadfast love to Abraham, as [he has] sworn to our fathers from the days of old" (7:20).

And what form will this faithfulness and love assume? In what ways will it be manifested? How will God's covenant people experience his mercy? This is where the good news of what God does with our sin comes into play. Says the prophet,

Who is a God like you, pardoning iniquity
and passing over transgression
for the remnant of his inheritance?
He does not retain his anger forever,
because he delights in steadfast love.
He will again have compassion on us;
he will tread our iniquities underfoot.
You will cast all our sins
into the depths of the sea. (vv. 18–19)

There are three things that this promise assures us God will do with our sin: he will pass over it, he will tread it underfoot, and he will cast all our sins into the depths of the sea. In this chapter, we turn our attention to the first of these, reserving the second and third for later.

Before we explore this glorious truth, we must not move too quickly past the question that Micah asks, "Who is a God like you?" The obvious answer is, "No one!" Although there are other "gods" of man's own making, idols and images in which he vainly invests power and to which he looks in hope, there is no God but our God. And he is peerless! He has no equal. None can even remotely compare to him. He is, quite literally, in a class by himself. Have we not seen this already in the numerous ways that God has dealt with our sin? Do we not see it in the indescribable gift he has made to us of his Son, Jesus Christ?

Micah's question could as easily be put in the form of a declaration: "There is no God like you! You are incomparable! You are beyond our wildest dreams and expectations of what we would want our God to be. You exceed our desires and transcend our imagination." It seems as if Micah anticipates the words of the apostle

Paul, who spoke of God as the one, the only one, "who is able to do far more abundantly than all that we ask or think" (Eph. 3:20).

So, what does Micah mean when he confidently declares that God passes over our transgressions? Perhaps the place to begin is with our common human experience. We all know what it means to "pass over" something in various circumstances. It is to pay no heed; it is to ignore; it is to act as if whatever is passed over is no longer present. But this doesn't mean God ignores or pretends that our sin never existed. As we have seen, and as we must always remember, the reason God passes over our sin is because he has laid it on Christ. He did not "pass over" Jesus when he hung on the cross. He lingered in wrath as the Son of God was exposed to judgment that we deserved. That is why now God always and forevermore will "pass over" our transgressions.

It's crucial that we understand what "pass over" does not mean. It does not mean that God is indifferent to our sin or that in the final analysis it just doesn't matter all that much. When I "pass over" the squash that comes my way at Thanksgiving dinner, it is because I hate it. I loathe its taste. I am not simply indifferent toward it; I despise it and want it to pass by me as quickly as possible. But this is not Micah's meaning. God takes seriously our sin. He is keenly aware of even the slightest of our transgressions. But he chooses to "pass over" them and not hold us accountable because his perfect justice has determined to exact sin's due punishment from our substitute, the Lord Jesus Christ.

I'm lingering on this point because our English words "pass over" can be misleading when it comes to what God has done with our sin. When I go shopping for a new winter coat, I "pass over" numerous options because they don't appeal to me. They either don't fit or are the wrong color or are made with a low-quality fabric. When an awkward and uncoordinated teenager is passed over as sides for a soccer game are being chosen, he feels the shame of being singled out as incompetent and unwanted. These notions of what it is to "pass over" something are what make it a challenge for us to fully appreciate what God has done when it comes to our wicked ways.

There are many today, as I took note earlier, who wish to repudiate any notion of penal substitutionary atonement. They believe it is entirely within God's character and power simply to forgive—willy-nilly, as it were. God, because he is God, can and will arbitrarily and without demanding that justice be served, pass over all our sin. Such, they say, is the grandeur of his love and mercy. Perhaps they think God should be like this because they are. It doesn't take all that much for us as humans to turn a blind eye to the countless ways people offend us. They think that as long as evil can be ignored, it should be. And isn't this what we mean when we speak of God being loving and merciful?

Well, of course God is loving and merciful. But he, unlike you and me, is also perfectly just and holy. And that is why, in the beautiful conjunction of love and justice, he provides in himself a sacrifice that satisfies his justice and gives expression to his love. The cross of Christ that makes it possible for God to "pass over" our sins is the consummate convergence of holiness and kindness, of retribution and relief, of wrath and mercy, of both adherence to the demands of divine law and abundant provision of divine tenderhearted compassion for lost souls.

Perhaps a brief word about the nature of retributive justice is called for. When we speak about the justice of God, we have in mind the idea that God always acts in perfect conformity and harmony with his own character. Some suggest that justice is thus a synonym for righteousness. Whatever God is, says, or does, by virtue of the fact that it is God, makes it righteous. Right and wrong are simply, and respectively, what God either commands or forbids. In other words, God doesn't do or command something because it is right. It is right because it is done or commanded by God. Righteousness or rectitude or good do not exist independently of God as a law or rule or standard to which God adheres or conforms. Rather, righteousness or rectitude or good are simply God acting and speaking.

This is bothersome to some, as they think it makes the existence of good and evil altogether arbitrary. No, it doesn't. It doesn't because what God declares as good is a reflection of his own nature. Good cannot be any different from what it is because God cannot be any different from who he is. His eternal and righteous character is consistently expressed in affirmations of what is good and evil. We know something is good because the God who declares it good is himself good. We likewise know something is evil because it is contrary to the holiness of God's nature. We need never fear that God will suddenly reverse himself and declare good to be evil or evil to be good, because for him to do so would entail his ceasing to be God. By definition, God is always good and never evil.

Justice, therefore, is God acting and speaking in conformity with who he is. To say that God is just is to say that he acts and speaks consistently with whatever his righteous nature requires. To be unjust is to act and speak inconsistently with whatever his righteous nature requires. That, of course, is a contradiction. That would be to assert that the righteous God acts unrighteously. By definition, that is impossible.

Our primary concern here is with what has been called the retributive justice of God, or that which God's nature requires him to require of his creatures. Retributive justice is that in virtue of which God gives to each of us that which is our due. It is that in virtue of which God treats us according to what we deserve. Retributive justice is thus somewhat synonymous with punishment. This is a necessary expression of God's reaction to sin and evil. Retributive justice is not something that God may or may not exercise, as is the case with mercy, love, and grace. Retributive justice (i.e., punishment for sin) is a matter of debt. It is something from which God cannot refrain doing, lest he violate the rectitude and righteousness of his nature and will. Sin must be punished. It is a serious misunderstanding of Christianity and the nature of forgiveness to say that believers are those whose guilt is rescinded and whose sins are not punished. Our guilt and sin were fully imputed to our substitute, Jesus, who suffered the retributive justice in our stead.

It's worth asking the question why people today object to the biblical portrayal of God as judge? Why is there such a visceral, angry reaction to the notion that God holds sinners accountable for their sin, thus requiring his offer of a substitutionary sacrifice, lest we all die eternally? Why do so many think that retributive judgment is unworthy of God? Have you paused to consider what kind of God our God would be if retributive judgment were not part of his character? J. I. Packer responded to this by asking,

> Would a God who did not care about the difference between right and wrong be a good and admirable Being? Would a God who put no distinction between the beasts of history, the Hitlers and Stalins (if we dare use names), and his own saints, be morally praiseworthy and perfect? Moral indifference would be an imperfection in God, not a perfection. But not to judge the world would be to show moral indifference. The final proof

that God is a perfect moral Being, not indifferent to questions of right and wrong, is the fact that he has committed himself to judge the world.[1]

Of course, I cannot let this statement pass without reaffirming yet again that it is possible for us to escape this global judgment, not on the assumption that God will simply ignore our sin and let bygones be bygones, but only if we will believe in the Lord Jesus Christ and put our faith in his having endured the penalty for sin that we otherwise would inevitably face.

Additional insight into what it means for God to pass over our transgressions is found in the explanatory declaration that God "does not retain his anger forever, because he delights in steadfast love" (Mic. 7:18). God's anger is not retained because it is vented on our substitute, Jesus Christ. It was the steadfast love of the Lord that prompted the sending of his Son to address the righteous anger of God against sin (see John 3:16).

There is yet additional evidence that the reason God passes over our transgressions is because the punishment due them was laid on Christ. We see this when we compare the proclamation in Micah 7 with the description of the Suffering Servant in Isaiah 53. There is remarkable and glorious overlap between the two. The Hebrew word in Micah 7:18 translated as "pardoning" appears in Isaiah 53:12 to describe how the Messiah "bore" the sin of many. The "iniquity" (Mic. 7:18) that God pardons is the very "iniquity" that has been "laid" on Christ (Isa. 53:6, 11). And the "transgression" (Mic. 7:18) that God passes over is again the "transgression" for which Messiah Jesus was "stricken" (Isa. 53:8, 12). The word ren-

---

1   J. I. Packer, *Knowing God* (Downers Grove, IL: IVP, 1993), 143.

dered to communicate that God "delights" (Mic. 7:18) in steadfast love is the very word that describes his "will" to crush Jesus in our place (Isa. 53:10).

When you find yourself burdened with guilt and regret and self-contempt for all the many ways you have failed your family and made sinful use of your eyes and greedily clutched to your wealth while the poor go without, remember what God has done with your sin: He has passed over it. He has not demanded that you pay the penalty but has been satisfied with the penalty that fell on Christ Jesus. And Jesus himself happily—yes, happily and joyfully and freely—took on himself the task of offering his own body and soul in your stead, enduring your judgment, tasting what it means in your place to be "forsaken" by the Father (Matt. 27:46), so that God might pass over your iniquities.

Thus, we see that when Micah celebrates the truth that God "passes over" our sins and transgressions, he means that God has chosen not to punish us for them, but rather his Son in our stead. God does not pardon our sin because he chose not to demand that his justice be served. It is precisely because justice is served and fully honored in the death of Jesus that he can look at our sin and pass over it.

9

He Has Trampled
Your Sin Underfoot

I WANT TO ASK YOU a series of questions, to each of which, in my opinion, there is one simple answer. Rest assured that I'm asking myself the same questions.

- What is the single greatest and most imposing obstacle to your enjoyment of God? What is it that causes you to doubt whether God truly delights in you as his child? What is it that deafens your spiritual ears to hear the Father singing in joy and heartfelt affection for you (see Zeph. 3:17)?
- What is it that leads you to shake your head with doubt and dismay when you read in Scripture of the commitment of Christ to his sheep?
- What, more than anything else, keeps you at arm's length from your heavenly Father? What is it that makes you think he is repulsed by you and that he takes offense at your very existence?

- What is it that makes you hesitant to draw near to God and to seek his help? Why do you instinctively run *from* him rather than *to* him when you sin?
- What is the primary reason why you don't pray more than you do? There is an underlying reason why you don't have confidence that God truly wants you to come boldly to the throne of grace to find mercy and grace to help you in your time of need (see Heb. 4:16). Do you know what it is?
- What is the primary reason that when you do pray, you live in fear and anxiety that God either won't hear it or, if he does hear it, won't answer it in the way you want him to? Why do you live in constant hesitancy when it comes to your prayers? What is it about your relationship with God that would lead you to question or perhaps even deny that he loves you enough to answer your prayers?
- Why are you restrained in your worship of God? What do you think is in the heart of God in relation to you when he sees you with hands raised and your heart engaged and your mouth proclaiming his greatness? What is it that stirs up images of God turning his back on you in disgust and disdain?
- Why are you reluctant to share your faith with non-Christians you know? What is it that causes you to think of yourself as unqualified to step up and serve in the local church?
- What is the primary cause of your fear, worry, doubt, and self-contempt? Simply put, there is a reason why you live largely devoid of the peace that Paul says transcends understanding and exceeds our greatest efforts to fathom (see Phil. 4:7). What is the reason?
- Why do you struggle to find energy and motivation to read your Bible on a regular basis? Do you doubt the truth of what

it proclaims? Do you think that its promises apply to everyone else but you? If so, why?

• Why are joy and peace so infrequent in your spiritual experience? When you read 1 Peter 1:8 and hear of a joy that is inexpressible and full of glory, do you see joy as an unattainable dream far beyond your grasp?

Now that, dear friend, is quite a list of questions! It virtually spans the spectrum of issues in the Christian life. And as you have come to see throughout the course of this book, I strongly believe that there is one answer to them all. The single overriding and most debilitating factor that threatens to undermine everything in our Christian lives and in our relationship with God is the failure to understand, embrace, and enjoy the full and final forgiveness of our sins. The reason you and I struggle to enjoy God is because we live in constant fear that he doesn't enjoy us. And how could he when our guilt and shame remain? And why do we experience this fear? Because we don't understand, embrace, and enjoy the pervasive teaching of Scripture concerning the many things that God has done with our sins!

The reason we are so hesitant to draw near to God and bring our prayerful requests to him is that we live in fear that he's angry with us. And why shouldn't he be when our misbehavior and indifference to him are so evident? And why do we experience this hesitation? Because we don't understand, embrace, and enjoy the fact that God has laid our sins on his Son, Jesus Christ.

The reason we feel uncomfortable in being entirely free and joyful and heartfelt in our worship is that we wonder whether God might still be disgusted with us. We worry that his wrath still abides on us and that we are still subject to eternal condemnation. The lingering memory of sins committed leads us to think that God looks at our worship and our service in the church as hypocritical. And why do we live in bondage to those crippling thoughts? Because we don't understand, embrace, and enjoy the fact that God has forgiven us of all our sins and placed them behind his back and cast them into the depths of the sea.

Now, am I exaggerating things a bit? Maybe. I suppose there are other reasons why we don't live our Christian lives the way we know we should and with the joy and energy and zeal that we would prefer. But I'm still convinced that deep down inside many Christian souls is the lingering fear, the ever-present doubt, the crippling uncertainty that God has all of our sins in the forefront of his mind and stands ready to use them against us.

Feelings of guilt, shame, and self-contempt pose the greatest threat to a robust and joyful Christian experience. Nothing serves to undermine the intimacy of our relationship with God quite like the piercing pain of guilt, the lingering memory of multiple moral failures in our past, and the darkness of shame that so often accompanies it. Simply put, our fundamental problem is that we either haven't heard or don't recall or simply refuse to believe what God has done with our sin. Will you believe it now?

Sin Stomped into the Dust

If you and I would wholeheartedly embrace the truth that our sins have been thoroughly crushed beneath the feet of Jesus, how might we answer the many questions asked above? Would not our zeal for holiness be heightened? Would not our passion for the Son of God be intensified? Would not our generosity be increased? Would not our sacrifice for the sake of others be expanded? Would not our hunger for the Scriptures be multiplied? Would not our prayer life be far more robust and consistent than it currently is? We know the answer. Yes!

So let's return once again to the prophecy of Micah, and dig considerably more deeply into this breathtaking declaration of what God has done with our sin. He has pardoned our iniquity, which is to say he has forgiven us. He has passed over our transgressions. Out of compassion for his people, he will cast all our sins into the ocean depths. And he will trample underfoot all our guilt, erasing it from view.

> Who is a God like you, pardoning iniquity
>   and passing over transgression
>   for the remnant of his inheritance?
> He does not retain his anger forever,
>   because he delights in steadfast love.
> He will again have compassion on us;
>   he will tread our iniquities underfoot.
> You will cast all our sins
>   into the depths of the sea. (Mic. 7:18–19)

The imagery here in Micah 7 is found throughout Scripture to describe the utter and altogether comprehensive defeat of one's enemies. To trample something underfoot is to put it in complete submission. One's authority and power to rule is expressed by the portrayal of one's feet driving all opposition and enmity into the dust. It is to put on display the victory you have achieved over whomever or whatever your enemy may be.

It was customary in ancient times for a military conquest to be vividly portrayed by the placing of the victor's foot on the neck of his defeated foe. The conquered general, assuming he survived the war, would lie prostrate on the ground, while the conquering general would trample him underfoot, driving his neck more deeply into the dirt. It was an unmistakable picture of both victory and defeat.

When the apostle Paul describes the triumph of Jesus Christ over all opposition, be it death, sin, Satan, and all demonic hosts, he does so by speaking of everything being placed under his feet. When Jesus was raised from the dead and seated at the right hand of the majesty on high, "far above all rule and authority and power and dominion, and above every name that is named, not only in this age but also in the one to come" (Eph. 1:20–21), God the Father "put all things under his feet and gave him as head over all things to the church, which is his body, the fullness of him who fills all in all" (vv. 22–23).

To be subjected beneath the feet of Jesus is to be placed under his authority, to be compelled to do his bidding, and ultimately to suffer defeat should there be any resistance to his sovereign sway. It certainly comes as no surprise, then, that Paul would describe the second coming of Christ and his victory over all opposition in precisely these terms. We read this in 1 Corinthians 15:

Then comes the end, when he delivers the kingdom to God the Father after destroying every rule and every authority and power. For he must reign until he has put all his enemies under his feet. The last enemy to be destroyed is death. For "God has put all things in subjection under his feet." (vv. 24–27)

Satan is no exception to this outcome, for Paul assures us all that "the God of peace will soon crush Satan under your feet" (Rom. 16:20). Does it strike you as odd that it is the God "of peace" who crushes Satan under our feet? Peace seems to be inconsistent with the violence expressed in the trampling of one's enemies underfoot. "But God's peace," says Stott, "allows no appeasement of the devil. It is only through the destruction of evil that true peace can be attained."[1] Even more remarkable is the fact that Satan—and, by extension, all his demonic hosts—"are crushed under the feet of believers, not the feet of Jesus. Such a scenario indicates that the victory of the Christ is shared with his followers so that the triumph of the Christ is also their triumph."[2]

When we bring this imagery to bear on the words of Micah 7, we are assured that our sin is forever and finally crushed into oblivion. Its power to condemn and control us has been overturned and reduced to dust. For God to tread underfoot all our sins means that he has utterly defeated them. Sin's power over you is done away with. Its authority to rule your life is undone (see Rom. 6:12). God has conquered the threat that sin poses. He has taken steps to eliminate any possibility that it might rise up at the judgment day to successfully indict us. It no longer has the capacity to steal your joy or undermine your value or determine your eternal destiny. And the way in which God goes about making this point and driving it home is by asking you to envision in your mind your sin on the ground, in the dirt, beneath his feet, as it were, as he treads upon it, stomping it into nothingness, rendering it impotent to separate you from his love in Christ.

1   John Stott, *Romans: God's Good News for the World* (Downers Grove, IL: InterVarsity Press, 1994), 401.
2   Thomas R. Schreiner, *Romans*, 2nd ed. (Grand Rapids, MI: Baker Academic, 2018), 779.

10

He Has Cast Your Sin into the Sea

WE NOTED PREVIOUSLY in Micah 7 two wonderful things God
has done to reconcile us to himself: he has passed over our transgressions and has tread our iniquities under his feet. Both transgressions and iniquities have been dealt with, and now God acts
to deal with our sins:

> Who is a God like you, pardoning iniquity
>   and passing over transgression
>   for the remnant of his inheritance?
> He does not retain his anger forever,
>   because he delights in steadfast love.
> He will again have compassion on us;
>   he will tread our iniquities underfoot.
> You will cast all our sins
>   into the depths of the sea. (vv. 18–19)

Hardly a week passes that I don't see somewhere on TV a showing of the epic film *Titanic* (1997). You know, the one starring

Leonardo DiCaprio and Kate Winslet. I have to admit I enjoyed the film when it first came out, but I studiously avoid watching it now, except for the opening ten minutes. It is during the first part of the movie that we are shown actual footage of the sunken super vessel. The Titanic was 882.5 feet long and 92.5 feet wide, and when fully laden, displaced more than 52,000 tons. Robert Ballard, who led an American/French expedition from aboard the United States Navy research ship Knorr, first discovered the wreck of the Titanic in August of 1985. Making use of the Argo, a 16-foot vessel with a remote-controlled camera, the first underwater images of the Titanic were seen on September 1, 1985. What remains of the Titanic is at the bottom of the Atlantic Ocean, approximately 13,000 feet underwater.

Now, let's apply this historic reality to the imagery we find in Micah 7. It is wonderfully good news to hear that God has cast all our sins into the depths of the sea. But some would push back and insist that the story of the Titanic reminds us that everything can eventually be found and seen once again. Might our sins likewise be discovered, elevated from the murky waters of our past, and brought back into play in our relationship with the Lord? Absolutely not! My point in sharing the details of the Titanic's demise and discovery is to remind us all that this will never, ever happen when it comes to our sins!

Let me make the point yet again. Our oceans together cover some 140,000,000 square miles, or 71 percent of the earth's surface. The average depth is 2.3 miles. The deepest waters occur in relatively narrow trenches. At present, the greatest depth is found in the Mariana Trench in the western region of the North Pacific Ocean, east of the Mariana Islands. It is 1,580 miles long, with an average width of 43 miles. Its deepest area is 6.85 miles (or approximately 36,201 feet). On January 23, 1960, Jacques Piccard made a record dive to 35,800 feet, some 400 feet shy of the literal bottom of the ocean floor.[1]

Might he have discovered our sins somewhere in the "depths" of that sea? No! Of course, I'm pressing the imagery in Micah 7:19 to make my point. Even should someone someday in some remarkably resilient underwater vessel touch the bottom of the Mariana Trench, no one will ever recover our sins and bring them to the surface. No one will ever succeed in making use of them to alienate us from God.

Let's return to the Old Testament prophet once again. Here in chapter 7, Micah draws upon Israel's history to make his point. Nothing weighed more joyfully on the minds of God's people than the story of how he delivered Israel from bondage in Egypt and then conquered Pharaoh and his armies by drowning them in the Red Sea. In other words, "Israel's sins are now implicitly personified as the pharaoh and his picked troops. Unless their sins are triumphantly 'subdued' and completely 'hurl[ed]' into the depths of the sea' (Ex. 15:4–5), the elect nation has no hope of liberation from the sin that enslaves them."[2] Listen carefully to the language of Exodus 15:4–5 that describes this incredible event:

> "Pharaoh's chariots and his host he cast into the sea,
>   and his chosen officers were sunk in the Red Sea.
> The floods covered them;
>   they went down into the depths like a stone."

1 Just for the sake of comparison, when measured by its height above sea level, Mt. Everest is the tallest mountain in the world at 29,035 feet above sea level.
2 Bruce K. Waltke, "Micah," in *The Minor Prophets: An Exegetical and Expository Commentary*, vol. 2, ed. Thomas Edward McComiskey (Grand Rapids, MI: Baker, 1993), 763.

There is simply no escaping the fact that Micah is appealing to this victory of God over the enemies of his people to portray what God does in defeating and subduing and forever setting us free from the guilt and punishment of our sin. Waltke makes this clear:

> Israel's liberation from the powerful Egyptians at the beginning of its history now becomes a type of its even greater spiritual salvation from enslaving sin in the future. All their sins are completely vanquished by God's grace and—as the rest of Scripture testifies—through the cross of Jesus Christ.[3]

How much more graphic must God be before you enter into the joy of his forgiving love? All vestige of condemning guilt is gone. Jerry Bridges drives home this point by reminding us that

> just as God said He *put* our sins behind His back, so here He says He will *hurl* them into the depths of the sea. They will not 'fall overboard'; God will hurl them into the depths. He wants them to be lost forever, because He has fully dealt with them in His Son, Jesus Christ.[4]

The submarine has not been made that can submerge to the depths where God has cast our sin. The equipment has not been found, and never will be, that can retrieve the slightest vestige of your transgressions. The camera does not exist that can capture an image of so much as a single transgression. God forbids it. Such is the quality of his forgiving love. Bridges makes the point yet again:

3 Waltke, "Micah," 762.
4 Jerry Bridges, *Transforming Grace: Living Confidently in God's Unfailing Love* (Colorado Springs, CO: Navpress, 1991), 40.

Do you begin to get the picture? Are you realizing that God's forgiveness is complete and irreversible? Have you started to understand that regardless of how "bad" you've been or how many times you've committed the same sin, God completely and freely forgives you because of Christ? Do you see that, because God has already dealt with your sins in Christ, you do not have to do penance or fulfill some probationary term before God can bless you or use you again?[5]

Nothing that I've said in this book, and certainly nothing that Micah wrote in his prophetic work, should be taken to mean that God doesn't take our sin seriously, as if he were little more than an overly indulgent and excessively permissive parent who lets his kids run wild without any restraints. As Bridges so aptly remind us, "in His relationship to us as our heavenly Father, God does deal with our sins, but only in such a way as for our good. He does not deal with us as our sins deserve, which would be punishment, but as His grace provides, which is for our good."[6]

Your Sin "Sleeps with the Fishes"

I'll close this chapter with an illustration from what may well be the greatest film ever produced: *The Godfather*. Of the many intriguing characters in the film, that of strong-armed hitman Luca Brasi was somewhat unique. The actor who portrayed Brasi was born Leonardo Passafaro (b. March 13, 1926; d. May 12, 1992). He later went by the name Lenny Montana. The six-feet, six-inches Montana had a successful career as a professional wrestler before he became an actor. Oddly enough, he was in real life an enforcer for

5 Bridges, *Transforming Grace*, 40–41.
6 Bridges, *Transforming Grace*, 40.

the Colombo crime family. Although it is never made clear in the film, one assumes that it was Brasi who placed the severed head of the horse, Khartoum, in the bed of that unfortunate Hollywood movie producer.

In any case, what concerns us here is Brasi's death. In the film, he is murdered while attempting to join forces with a rival crime family. Later, as the Corleone family considers how to respond to the attempted murder of their leader, Vito Corleone, a package arrives. In it is a dead fish, wrapped in the bulletproof vest previously worn by Brasi. "What's this," asks Sonny Corleone? "It means Luca Brasi sleeps with the fishes," explains Clemenza.

Clearly, Luca Brasi's body had been weighted down and cast into some river, bay, or more likely the Atlantic Ocean, never to be seen again. His body would never float to the surface and serve as evidence against those who killed him. His remains had sunk to the bottom and were permanently out of sight, beyond recovery.

Yes, it's a graphic image, perhaps too unpleasant to be included in a book of this sort. But the portrayal in Micah 7 of what God has done with our sin calls for every analogy and explanation available to us. Those who murdered Luca Brasi and disposed of his body did so from hatred and greed, and perhaps a measure of fear. But when God cast our sins into the immeasurable depths of the sea, he did so out of his great love with which he loved us. His design was that every trace or residual evidence of our immorality and idolatry and selfish unbelief would be forever banished.

If I may say this reverently, there is a far greater probability that the body of Luca Brasi will rise to the surface than will your sins. The entire history of your failures and the guilt of your transgressions sleeps with the fishes. You need never fear that a fisherman or deep-sea diver or Satan or even your worst enemy in life will be successful in retrieving the remains of your disobedience and making use of it to accuse you in the courtroom of heaven. Such is one more thing that God has done with your sin.

11

He Has Blotted Out Your Sin

MANY OF US HAVE THE IDEA in our heads and hearts that when God writes, he does so with indelible ink. In one particular case, that's true. When God wrote our names in the Lamb's book of life before the foundation of the world, he did so in a manner that those names would be permanently and irreversibly recorded. Jesus himself promised that "the one who conquers will be clothed thus in white garments, and I will never blot his name out of the book of life" (Rev. 3:5; cf. 13:8; 17:8).

But there is another kind of "blotting out" that we must consider. And in this case, it is indescribably good news that God will indeed blot out our sins and transgressions, leaving no trace behind of their commission or their capacity to render us liable for condemnation. We see this in several texts of Scripture. For example,

> "I, I am he
>   Who *blots out* your transgressions for my own sake,
>   and I will not remember your sins." (Isa. 43:25)

In this instance, notes Old Testament scholar John Oswalt, "what [God] does is to erase from the record every trace of the transgression and sin of his people, not once but continually and forever so that he cannot remember it."[1] This is an expression not of our value or worth but an expression of his nature, as he does it for his own sake. Nothing Israel has done or can do, Oswalt explains, "can qualify them for forgiveness like this. If God did not wish to do it, no court could require him to do so, and no power could compel him. It is purely an expression of the gracious character of him who is at the center of all things, encompasses all things, and is beyond all things."[2] Oswalt acknowledges that nothing is said here of the "means" by which God can do this, but "it will later be shown how the ministry of the Servant will make such an action consistent with the justice and honor of God (53:10–12)."[3] And again,

> "I have *blotted out* your transgressions like a cloud
>   and your sins like a mist;
> return to me, for I have redeemed you." (44:22)

In the case of Isaiah 44:22, the meaning is that "as real and substantial as sin is, God has the power to remove it from the record as swiftly as a rising wind can sweep a cloud from the sky."[4] Twice in Psalm 51, David employs this imagery in his prayer for forgiveness:

> Have mercy on me, O God,
>   according to your steadfast love;

1 John N. Oswalt, *The Book of Isaiah, Chapters 40–66* (Grand Rapids, MI: Eerdmans, 1998), 160.
2 Oswalt, *The Book of Isaiah*, 160–61.
3 Oswalt, *The Book of Isaiah*, 161.
4 Oswalt, *The Book of Isaiah*, 188.

according to your abundant mercy
blot out my transgressions. (v. 1)

Hide your face from my sins,
and *blot out* all my iniquities. (v. 9)

David envisions his sins written down by God in a book that he keeps constantly up to date. Each day, with each moral failure or ill-advised word or jealous impulse or lustful thought, God writes it down and revisits it to keep it fresh in his mind. Unlike a modern computer that has a delete key, this book is handwritten by the Creator and Judge himself. There will be no mistake on judgment day, no possibility that anything was omitted or overlooked. It will be right there, written in what feels like indelible ink, unless, of course, God in mercy and sovereign grace chooses to "blot" it out.

Consider what we so often see in either top-secret documents or legal papers in which the names of certain individuals or other pertinent facts are blotted out by a solid black line. Such information is considered too sensitive to be made public. It is thus eliminated from view by a deliberate act of the court or some authorized individual. Although the analogy isn't perfect, it makes the point. Our sins cannot be read. They cannot be admitted into court as evidence to secure a conviction. God has effectively blotted out every trace of transgression or spiritual crime.[5]

Learning Theology from a Child's Toy

Have you ever fooled around with an Etch A Sketch? (I just dated myself!) It's that toy with what looks like a television screen and

---

5 The appeal made by Peter on the day of Pentecost contains the same picture: "Repent therefore, and turn back, that your sins may be blotted out" (Acts 3:19).

two knobs that enable you to sketch whatever fits your fancy. I never was much good at it. I'm not an artist by any stretch of the imagination. The Etch A Sketch was made for people like me. If you don't like what you've drawn—and especially don't want to be embarrassed, should anyone else see it—you simply shake the screen, and your work of art vanishes!

It's a crude and simple illustration, but that is a lot like what God does with your sin when he grants forgiveness. Through the course of our earthly existence we sketch an ugly scenario of sin and rebellion and ingratitude and jealousy and lust. There it is, vividly imprinted on the screen of our souls. But when we confess our sin, as David did, God's loving and gracious hand tips the toy and the slate is wiped clean! No matter how often we return to deface our lives with ugly pictures of hatred and anger and pride and envy, God is faithful to shake the screen. All it takes is confession. All it takes is the blood of Christ.

Expunged!

Please don't take what I'm about to say as boasting, but by God's grace, I have never been cited for speeding. Never. I've been driving since I was sixteen years old, and my record is completely clean. Well, sort of. No, more than sort of. Let me explain.

When I was a senior in high school, back in 1969, I was dating a young lady who was only a sophomore. Given the fact that the prom each year was designed for only seniors and juniors, she wasn't able to attend. So we made use of her father's car to drive from Duncan, Oklahoma, where we both lived, to Oklahoma City for dinner and a movie. On the drive back home, just south of Chickasha, Oklahoma, I was pulled over by a state trooper. When I first spotted him, I looked closely at the speedometer. It read fifty-five miles per hour. You need to understand that in 1969, in Oklahoma, the speed limit was fifty-five miles per hour. I realize that most reading this book will be stunned by that fact, but it is true, nonetheless.

As it turned out, the speedometer on the car was faulty and registered approximately ten miles per hour fewer than what I was actually traveling. Yes, it would have been nice if my girlfriend's father had informed me of this, but alas. So I was ticketed. But that's not the end of the story.

The alleged offense took place in a county where my father's childhood best friend was the district attorney. My dad made a phone call to him the following day and explained the circumstances under which I was cited for speeding. I am grateful to this day for the district attorney's decision to expunge the speeding ticket from my record. I love that word *expunge*! Synonyms include "to strike out," "obliterate," "delete," and "completely erase." But the synonym I love the most is "to blot out."

Legally speaking, therefore, I have never been cited for breaking the law. "You must be terribly boring, Sam," some of you may be tempted to say. No, not boring, just law-abiding! But the important point to note is that the blotting out or expunging of that alleged offense was a legal action. I still carry the memory of that night. But as far as the law of the land is concerned, it never happened. All traces of its existence are gone, wiped clean from the books. Praise God![6]

Such is precisely what God has done with our sins. He has expunged them from the record. There is no evidence of such sins

---

6 Okay, in the interests of complete transparency, I have been pulled over a couple of times. But in each instance, I was able to persuade the officer that, contrary to what his radar had registered, I was innocent (and I was)! Once again, praise be to God!

ever having been committed. They are wiped clean and eradicated with such decisive finality that you and I will never be held accountable or judged for them, ever. Not in this life or in the life to come. Never.

Permanent Record?

When twenty-nine-year-old Edward Snowden fled to Hong Kong in June of 2013 with a plethora of top-secret NSA (National Security Agency) and CIA (Central Intelligence Agency) documents, as well as information on the activity of the British intelligence agency GCHQ (Government Communications Headquarters), he created a firestorm of controversy that still rages. My comments here are not designed to either defend or indict him. He has many on his side who are convinced that what he did was heroic and much needed. Others have charged him with being a traitor. In fact, the United States government has charged him with three counts under the Espionage Act. But I take no sides. He currently resides with his wife in Moscow where he has been given asylum.

What I find of profound interest, and especially helpful in illustrating what the Bible says that God has done with our sins, is Snowden's disclosure that virtually every digital communication made by US citizens—be they text messages, Skype calls, emails, Facebook posts, phone calls, Google searches, credit card purchases, or the like—is part of what he calls a permanent record.[7] Snowden brought to the attention of the American public that there was little in their lives that they might reasonably regard as private. This permanent record of their movements, purchases,

---

7 *Permanent Record* (New York: Metropolitan Books, 2019), is the title to Snowden's recent, bestselling autobiographical account of what he did and why.

internet activity, and virtually all forms of communication and digital interaction with other people will likely never disappear, at least not in our lifetime. It will always be there for the NSA and the CIA to see and make use of, if they so choose. It is frightening, to say the least.[8]

But I worry far less about any record the government might permanently possess than I do about the possibility that God has made a permanent record of my wicked choices, thoughts, fantasies, and failures. The mere thought that my sins are forever registered in the mind of God or written down in some celestial volume is far more unsettling and disturbing to me than knowing that my government knows as much as it does.

And yet here is the good news. God keeps no such record! Nothing of my sin is written, typed, or recorded, either digitally or manually, or simply held by God in his infinite memory bank. God has mercifully blotted it out.

I don't know if it is even possible for certain government agencies to push delete and wipe from the record the massive amount of data that they currently hold on citizens of the US. My best guess is that even if they possess the capability of doing so, they never will. But God can. And God has. He has blotted out, expunged, eradicated, and canceled every last vestige of the condemning guilt of my transgressions. Yours too, if you know and trust Christ. I know that I've said it numerous times already, yet I need to remind us yet again. This did not happen because God sovereignly and arbitrarily pushed a button or destroyed the heavenly server on which this record was stored. Instead, he took the guilt of our sin

---

8 I should point out that the government's justification for this activity was their claim that it was essential to protect American citizens from future terrorist attacks such as those that occurred on September 11, 2001.

and imputed it to Jesus. There was a legal transference of the condemnation our sin deserved from us to him, and in the propitiatory, wrath-assuaging death of our Savior, all trace of anything that might otherwise be held against us is gone.

For Whose Sake?

Before we leave this glorious truth, something must be said about the ultimate motivation in God's heart. We have to look closely at *why* he has chosen to blot out our sins. For the answer, look again at Isaiah 43:25:

> "I, I am he
>   who blots out your transgressions *for my own sake*,
>   and I will not remember your sins."

I think I know your immediate reaction. It's mine too. To say that God blots out our sin for his own sake sounds rather selfish. Why wouldn't God do it for "our" sake? Well, in one sense, he does. It is obviously to our immeasurable advantage and for our sake that God blots out all of our sin and guilt. But as we've already noted, the blotting out of our sin is not the greatest and most blessed fruit of God's saving action. It is a good and glorious blessing only because it removes the primary obstacle to us getting God. The best news of all is that God has done everything necessary to eliminate every barrier to our experience of him. What good is the removal of our sin if it leaves us bereft of the most exquisite gift of all: knowing and seeing and enjoying God? Let me unpack this in a bit more detail.

Although it strikes many as wacky when they first hear it, the greatest and most intense passion in the heart of God is the glory of God. If it weren't, it would be meaningless to speak of his love for us. Why, you ask?

God's love for us is measured by the quality of what he gives us. If he is truly to love us—that is, to love us maximally and optimally—he must give us the very best he has. And the very best he has is *himself*! God's love for us is thus seen preeminently when he does whatever is necessary to give us himself and to awaken our hearts to the incomparable joy of honoring him as God and praising him for who he is. Now, does that sound like God loving himself? Yes. Does it sound like God seeking his own glory? Yes. Does it sound like God doing all he does for his own sake? Yes. And yet it is simultaneously God loving us in the most consummate and perfect way possible. The only way it is not an expression of God's love for us is if there is something more beautiful than God with which he can captivate our hearts. But there isn't. The only way it is not an expression of God's love for us is if there is something or someone more satisfying, more pleasing, more fascinating, more enthralling than God himself. But there isn't.

That is the simplest way of saying that when God seeks his own glory or does everything for his own sake, he is acting out of his love for you and me.

We see this numerous places in Scripture. One of them is the most famous of all the psalms:

> He restores my soul.
> He leads me in paths of righteousness
> *for his name's sake.* (Ps. 23:3)

Furthermore, we read this in Psalm 79:

Help us, O God of our salvation,
for the glory of your name;
deliver us, and atone for our sins,
for your name's sake. (v. 9)

Or consider 1 Samuel 12:22, where we read,

The LORD will not forsake his people, *for his great name's sake,*
because it has pleased the LORD to make you a people for himself.

God's undying commitment to you—to bless you, to save you, and to give you himself—is grounded in his undying commitment to glorify himself by enabling you to enjoy him forever. Here are several other texts that assert the same truth:

Remember not the sins of my youth or my transgressions;
according to your steadfast love remember me,
for the sake of your goodness, O LORD!" (Ps. 25:7)

For your name's sake, O LORD,
pardon my guilt, for it is great. (v. 11)

But you, O GOD my Lord,
deal on my behalf *for your name's sake;*
because your steadfast love is good, deliver me! (109:21)

"Though our iniquities testify against us,
act, O LORD, *for your name's sake;*
for our backslidings are many;
we have sinned against you." (Jer. 14:7)

I am writing to you, little children,
  because your sins are forgiven *for his name's sake*.
  (1 John 2:12)

"These things seem to show," wrote Jonathan Edwards, "that the salvation of Christ is for God's name's sake. Leading and guiding in the way of safety and happiness, restoring the soul, the forgiveness of sin, and that help, deliverance and salvation that is consequent thereon, is *for God's name*."[9]

When we come across a variety of texts that describe God's setting free his people from bondage in Egypt and again from captivity in Babylon, we read:

"And who is like your people Israel, the one nation on earth whom God went to redeem to be his people, *making himself a name* and doing for them great and awesome things." (2 Sam. 7:23)

Yet he saved them *for his name's sake*,
  that he might make known his mighty power. (Ps. 106:8)

who caused his glorious arm
  to go at the right hand of Moses,
who divided the waters before them
  to make for himself an everlasting name. (Isa. 63:12)

"But I [God] acted *for the sake of my name*, that it should not be profaned in the sight of the nations among whom they lived, in

9 Jonathan Edwards, *Dissertation Concerning the End for Which God Created the World*, in *The Works of Jonathan Edwards*, vol. 8, *Ethical Writings*, ed. Paul Ramsey (New Haven, CT: Yale University Press, 1989), 493.

whose sight *I made myself known* to them in bringing them out of the land of Egypt." (Ezek. 20:9)

"But I [God] acted *for the sake of my name*, that it should not be profaned in the sight of the nations." (v. 14)

"But I withheld my hand and acted *for the sake of my name*, that it should not be profaned in the sight of the nations." (v. 22)

Note the unashamed, unabashed repetitive proclamation of this truth in these texts:

> "*For my name's sake* I defer my anger;
>   *for the sake of my praise* I restrain it for you,
>   that I may not cut you off.
> Behold, I have refined you, but not as silver;
>   I have tried you in the furnace of affliction.
> For my own sake, for my own sake,[10] I do it,
>   for how should *my name* be profaned?
> *My glory* I will not give to another." (Isa. 48:9–11)

"But *I had concern for my holy name*, which the house of Israel had profaned among the nations to which they came.

"Therefore say to the house of Israel, Thus says the Lord GOD: It is not for your sake, O house of Israel, that I am about to act, but *for the sake of my holy name*, which you have profaned among the nations to which you came. And *I will vindicate the holiness of my great name*, which has been profaned among the

---

10 I did not mistakenly double-type that phrase.

nations, and which you have profaned among them. And *the nations will know that I am the* LORD, declares the Lord GOD, when through you I vindicate my holiness before their eyes'" (Ezek. 36:21–23; cf. Ezek. 29:16; 39:25; Dan. 9:19).

I know what you might be thinking. How can God love himself and his own glory with such energy and still love me? I said it earlier, but let me say it again in slightly different terms. Your greatest good and most intense pleasure can come only from enjoying the most excellent and exquisite Being in the universe. And that, of course, is God. And that enjoyment reaches its consummate expression only when you celebrate him in worship. In that way, God seeking his own glory and God seeking your greatest good are one and the same endeavor. I first learned this truth from C. S. Lewis,[11] who pointed out that all enjoyment tends towards praise and adoration as its appointed end. In this way, God's seeking his own glory (or doing everything "for his name's sake") and God's seeking your good converge. That, I can say with all confidence, is how God loves you.

---

11 See the chapter "A Word About Praising" in his book *Reflections on the Psalms* (New York: Harcourt Brace Jovanovich, 1958).

12

He Has Turned His Face
Away from Your Sin

WE'VE ALREADY HAD OCCASION to look at Psalm 51 and the way David portrays God dealing with his sin. He pleaded with God to "blot out" his transgressions, to "wash" him thoroughly from his iniquity, and to "cleanse" him from his sin (vv. 1–2). As if that were not enough, David then implores, "Hide your face from my sins" (v. 9).

We are dealing once again, as I noted earlier, with an anthropomorphism. God portrays himself as if he had a face. Eventually, the second person of the Godhead will assume human flesh in the person of Jesus and have not just a face but a fully formed human frame. But here, God is envisioned as if he had a face with eyes that can either look intently on our sins or, conversely, turn away and never see them again.

Perhaps the best way to understand what David is asking of God is to contrast it with what happens when God in judgment chooses to look intensely at the sins of his people. An especially graphic example of this is found in Jeremiah 16. There we read of the rampant idolatry of Israel (in particular, the southern kingdom of Judah) and the impending deportation of the nation into Babylon. The severity of Israel's sin and the judgment of God is seen in the graphic language of verse 18: "I will doubly repay their iniquity and their sin," says the Lord, "because they have polluted my land with the carcasses of their detestable idols, and have filled my inheritance with their abominations."

It may be that the people had grown so hardened in their sin and indifferent to God's law that they assumed the Lord simply failed to take notice of their ways. He was blindly oblivious to their transgressions, or so they thought. But the Lord counters their presumption by declaring, "For my eyes are on all their ways. They are not hidden from me, nor is their iniquity concealed from my eyes" (v. 17).

We find similar language in the prophecy of Amos. The prophet tells of how he saw the Lord standing beside the altar, pronouncing his determination to bring judgment on the rebellious nation. Even "if they hide themselves on the top of Carmel," declares the Lord, "from there I will search them out and take them; and if they hide from my sight at the bottom of the sea, there I will command the serpent, and it shall bite them" (Amos 9:3). When they go into captivity, says the Lord, "I will fix my eyes upon them / for evil and not for good" (v. 4).

It is simply impossible for the unrepentant and idolatrous to hide from God's sight. The Lord will "search them out" and "fix" his "eyes upon them." His "eyes are on all their ways," and no one can successfully hide from him or conceal their wickedness. David certainly knew this about God, which adds force and urgency to his appeal that God not look on his sin, that he "hide" his face from his wicked ways (Ps. 51:9).

Thus, we see that just as the eyes of the Lord are fixed on the rebellious ways of an unrepentant and defiant people, he turns his eyes away from the sins of the broken and contrite. We can rejoice and rest in the truth that our iniquity is now and forever "concealed" from the "eyes" of the Lord, not because he chooses merely to "wink" at sin but because he has looked on his Son as guilty of the spiritual crimes that we have committed.

So let's be clear about what David requests of the Lord. His plea is that God would not look any longer on his failures! Let not your eyes gaze on my wickedness! Perhaps the best way to understand this is to consider the many reasons why we look away from some event or person.

There have been times in my life—as in yours too, I'm sure—when I looked away because of the embarrassment I was feeling. I turned my face in the other direction, lest I set my eyes on something that I found to be emotionally discomfiting. This is not why God turned his face away from our sins. He's not embarrassed by us. He knows us thoroughly. No, his decision not to look on our sins is because he has cast his condemning gaze on another.

We often hide our eyes out of fear. Whether it is something or someone that we perceive to be a threat to our welfare or a sight that poses danger, we either look away or throw our hands up to cover our face. Not God. That is not what David is describing in this psalm.

People often laugh at me, in a good-natured sort of way, when I tell them that I hate monsters or disfigured creatures. Don't take offense at this, but I couldn't bring myself to watch any of *The Lord of the Rings* films. Images of distorted faces and physical ugliness tend to embed themselves in my mind and linger long. This explains why I can't bring myself to watch certain TV shows like *The Walking Dead* or any movie from the horror genre. God is surely not as easily offended at such sights as I am.

There are also numerous occasions in life when we feel utterly indifferent toward an individual or an incident and we choose to turn our faces away simply because we don't care. God cares. In fact, as we'll see, he turns his face away from our sin precisely because he cares passionately for us and is determined that our sins not adversely affect our relationship to him.

A reaction that is distinctly human, and no part of God's experience, is shame and how it leads us to hang our heads and divert our eyes away from the gaze of others. One of the more instructive occasions in which this is seen again concerns David. He himself describes it for us in Psalm 3.[1] Here are the first four verses:

> O LORD, how many are my foes!
>   Many are rising against me;
> many are saying of my soul,
>   "There is no salvation for him in God."
>
> But you, O LORD, are a shield about me,
>   my glory, and the lifter of my head.
> I cried aloud to the LORD,
>   and he answered me from his holy hill.

David's head was bowed low. He couldn't bring himself to lift his face and gaze upon anyone. Shame had virtually swallowed up his soul. But why? Here is the backstory to this time in David's life.

---

1   Much of what follows is adapted from my book *More Precious Than Gold: 50 Daily Meditations on the Psalms* (Wheaton, IL: Crossway, 2009), 29–33.

Absalom was David's third son. His second son, Chileab, is never mentioned after reference to his birth, leading us to assume that he died early on. David's firstborn son was Amnon. The story of how Amnon died is a sordid one. Amnon raped his half-sister, Tamar, and Absalom, Tamar's brother, swore revenge. It took two years, but Absalom finally arranged for Amnon to be killed. Fearing punishment, Absalom went into exile for three years. When he finally returned to Jerusalem, David refused to see him. Two more years passed before David and his son were reunited (although, even then, they weren't reconciled).

Absalom's plot to take the throne from his father probably emerged gradually. He began by currying favor with the people (2 Sam. 15:1–6). He portrayed himself as one who was interested in people by telling them he was far more capable of helping them with their troubles and securing justice for their complaints than was David. According to 2 Samuel 15:6, "Absalom stole the hearts of the men of Israel."

Once he felt secure in his position, he made his move. He went to Hebron, assembled his followers, and had himself anointed king (vv. 7–12). With a considerable army behind him, he marched against his father in Jerusalem and forced David to flee (vv. 13–17). Following a shameful period of absence from his throne, the armies of David eventually prevailed. Absalom was killed, contrary to his father's express wishes, serving only to intensify the latter's pain.

What an amazing scene: David, driven from his throne, subjected to indescribable humiliation, not by a pagan Gentile king but *by his own son!* Absalom's treachery and rebellion must have crushed David's heart. Here is the important point: it was while David was fleeing the armies of Absalom, broken by the spiteful betrayal of his own child, that he sat down and wrote the words of Psalm 3.

It wasn't while he sat on a golden throne with servants at his beck and call. It wasn't while lying on satin sheets and a soft pillow knowing that all was well with his family and among his people. Rather, it was in the midst of his most devastating and desperate hour that he penned these remarkable words:

> But you, O LORD, are a shield about me,
>   my glory, and *the lifter of my head.* (v. 3)

David's anguish was no doubt magnified by the fact that his adversaries were primarily from among his own people. Those once closest to him, those in whom he had once placed his confidence and trust, are now among those whose accusations are most bitter and hateful.

One of the primary tactics of such enemies is to undermine our faith in God to help us. David may well have been taunted with statements like: "If God is so good and so great, how come *we've* got the upper hand? How come *you're* on the run, David? Where is your God now, when you need him most?"

Perhaps they began to throw David's sin back in his face: his relationship with Bathsheba, the murder of Uriah, his failure as a father to Amnon and Absalom, and more. "God's not going to put up with that sort of thing, David. He's abandoned you for sure!" Yet, in the midst of such affliction, accusation, and abandonment, David's cry is for the "LORD," Yahweh, the covenant-keeping God (v. 1). David obviously knew that the hypnotic and paralyzing power of the enemy is broken only by turning one's gaze back to God. So he encourages himself by recalling three things about God, the last of which is especially important for us here.

First, God is a "shield" about him (Pss. 3:3; cf. 18:2, 30; 28:7; 33:20; 84:11; 91:4; 115:9–11). Second, God is his "glory" (3:3). This is probably David's way of saying, "I have no glory of my own. I put no trust in my fame or fortune. You alone, O God, are the joy, boast, and glory of my life."

Third, and most important of all, God is the one who "lifts his head" (v. 3). David left Jerusalem not only defeated but dejected, despondent, depressed. He hung his head in shame (2 Sam. 15:30). But he is confident that God will elevate his face and restore his hope.

When people are shy or unsure of themselves, perhaps due to some insecurity or recent failure, they rarely look up or make eye contact with others. Their aim is to pass by without being noticed. They hug the wall, lest a personal encounter expose their shame. Their deep feelings of inadequacy lead to withdrawal and silence. The last thing they want is to see or be seen. Fixing their eyes on the floor is safety for their soul. Embarrassment always expresses itself in a physical posture that is guarded and cautious.

David was probably having doubts about himself: about the validity of his calling, about his capacity or worthiness to rule Israel, about his worth as a man. Abasalom's treachery inflicted a depth of humiliation the human soul was never built to endure. It was emotionally crippling and threatened to destroy David's credibility and his confidence as a man after God's own heart.

Some of you know exactly how David felt. In your case, it may have been a stinging defeat, an embarrassing failure, or perhaps a public humiliation that you fear has forever destroyed your usefulness or your value to God or a place in his purposes. It's a devastating feeling. The enemy will often exploit the opportunity by reminding you of virtually every sin you've committed, reinforcing the painful conviction that you are now beyond recovery, hopelessly helpless, a stain on the public face of the church.

It might even be the rebellion of a child, as in the case of David. For some it's the demise of a business venture into which you poured every ounce of energy and income. Or it might be something less catastrophic, but no less painful, such as a failed attempt at public ministry or an embarrassing misstep that left you feeling exposed and unprotected.

In David's case, despite this crushing blow at the hands of his son, his faith in God never wavered, or at least not so as to throw him into utter despair. There was always and only One who was able to restore his strength and straighten his body and give him reason to hold his head high. This isn't arrogance or presumption or fleshly defiance, but humble wholehearted assurance that God can do for us what we can't do for ourselves. People often say, "I just can't bear to look anyone in the face after this." But God will make you able! He is the Lord who "makes poor and makes rich; he brings low and he exalts. He raises up the poor from the dust; he lifts the needy from the ash heap to make them sit with princes and inherit a seat of honor" (1 Sam. 2:7–8).

Yes, indeed, said David,

He will hide me in his shelter
   in the day of trouble;
he will conceal me under the cover of his tent;
   he will lift me high upon a rock.

And now my head shall be lifted up
   above my enemies all around me,
and I will offer in his tent

sacrifices with shouts of joy;
I will sing and make melody to the LORD. (Ps. 27:5–6)

My point in citing this story is simply to say that God never hangs his head or turns his face away from you and me because he is ashamed of us. In fact, when God turns his face away from our sins, it is precisely because he loves us and rejoices in our relationship to him as our Father. You and I may, like David, find ourselves hanging our heads and reluctant to set our eyes on anyone else, but God isn't. His determination not to look upon our repeated failures is driven by a deep and abiding passion for us and a desire to do us only good.

There may yet be one more thing in David's mind when he rejoices in knowing that God has turned his face away from his sin. We often speak of the importance of so-called eyewitness testimony. In the Old Testament, two or more eyewitnesses were required for a conviction. Could it be that God turns his face away because he declines to bear witness against us? It isn't that we aren't guilty; rather, God's mercy is seen in the fact that he is now blind to our faults, unable to make use of them to condemn us. And all this only because he has truly turned his face toward Jesus in judgment in our place. He sees our sin on his Son, and in doing so, his justice is satisfied.

This, then, is the gloriously good news of the gospel, that in the case of those whose trust is in Christ, God forever and finally has turned away his face away from all our transgressions. He cannot see them. He does not cast so much as a passing glance at our sin.

13

He Has Forgotten Your Sin and Refuses to Remember It

TRY TO FORGET, and I guarantee that you'll remember. Try to remember, and many times you'll find that you've forgotten. That's just how the human brain works. It's something that often drives me nuts. Incidents from my past that I thought I had long since banished from conscious thought, come racing back into the forefront of my thinking at the strangest times. Then there are those occasions when I can't remember where, five minutes before, I placed my car keys.

It all reminds me of a funny incident that my wife and I experienced several years ago. The incident has now led to an oft-repeated game that always causes us to laugh. We were driving somewhere, at some time in the past (I can't remember where or when), and the topic of 1960s TV came up in our conversation. We began to reminisce about a show that featured various rock and roll groups and a lot of girls dancing in the background. We wracked our brains for the name of the show, but nothing came to mind. About an hour later, it happened. Suddenly the name leapt into my head, and I shouted out loud, "Shindig!" I can't recall when Ann was so excited. We laughed and made fun of ourselves. To this day, when one of us suddenly remembers something that we thought we had long since forgotten, we shout out loud, "Shindig!" It's obviously an in-house Storms joke.

In any case, it does raise the question of memory and how we make use of it, or in many cases, abuse it. I've dealt with a lot of women who were abused in their younger years, only to suppress the memory of the trauma and then suffer when it comes rushing back into their heads. Most people I know confess that, as much as they may try, they can't shake the memory of those times when they were betrayed or violated or treated unjustly in some manner. It's as if such painful incidents have been seared into their brains with indelible ink. Such is the human condition.

But what about God? We know from multiple texts in the Bible that God is omniscient. If you're not familiar with that word, it literally means "all knowing." To be omniscient means you know everything—literally. Nothing escapes your gaze. Once something has happened, you never forget it. Of course, none of us knows what that's like. God alone, by virtue of being God, knows everything—past, present, and, yes, even the future. He knows it perfectly. He does not have partial knowledge that someone else can fill in on his behalf. What he knows—and he knows everything—he knows exhaustively. He knows why it happened, what it is, where and when it occurred, and everything that has resulted from it. He doesn't need anyone to inform him or bring him up to speed on events that we think he was too busy to notice. As David said in Psalm 139,

O Lord, you have searched me and known me!
You know when I sit down and when I rise up;
  you discern my thoughts from afar.
You search out my path and my lying down
  and are acquainted with all my ways.
Even before a word is on my tongue,
  behold, O Lord, you know it altogether. (vv. 1–4)

That being said, what possible sense could it make to say that God has forgotten our sins? How can the biblical author quote God as saying, "I, I am he / who blots out your transgressions for my own sake, / and *I will not remember your sins*" (Isa. 43:25)? Can God truly forget something? Is it possible in the most literal sense of the term for God not to "remember" what I've done? Well, no.

How utterly different from us is God! When people violate our rights or transgress us or defraud us or lie to us or break a promise, we make it clear to them: "I'll *never* forget this. I'll never let *you* forget this. I'll remember this to my dying day. I'll make sure I keep this in the forefront of my mind forever and I'll throw it in your face every chance I get." God, on the other hand, promises never to remember. He will not brood over our sin. He will not reflect upon it, think about it, contemplate it, analyze it, or ever again bring it up to himself, to you, or to others.

In other words, our fundamental problem is that we either haven't heard, don't recall, or simply refuse to believe what God said in Jeremiah 31:34, words that are quoted in Hebrews 10:17: "I will remember their sins and their lawless deeds no more" (cf. Heb. 8:12).

What haunts us and brings torment and unrest to our hearts is that we live as if those final two words weren't in the text. If I could provide a more emphatic translation, God is saying, "I will never again, by no means ever, remember their sins or lawless deeds."

What we feel deep inside is that God is constantly examining us, indicting us, and declaring to us: "I *will* remember their sins and their lawless deeds; I'll never forget," when in fact that is precisely what he declares he will do "no more"! No more! By which he means, "Never again! Never again!"

Even those who profess no faith at all in Jesus and operate on the basis of secular principles and a humanistic framework for understanding human nature will tell you that one of the most severely debilitating problems that anyone can face is guilt. Feelings of guilt can paralyze, intimidate, and suffocate the human soul. Feelings of guilt destroy marriages and drive people to a multitude of sinful alternatives. Psychologists who largely reject the biblical gospel still agree with us that guilt, self-condemnation, and contempt for one's own soul are perhaps the most problematic issues that people face.

But the great difference is that we who believe the word of God do not tell such people that they need to recognize that they *aren't* guilty. The answer isn't to say, "Look, your problem is that you are in bondage to false guilt. You shouldn't feel that way about yourself. You've done nothing to warrant this sort of mental and emotional agony."

Christians, on the other hand, say, "Your problem isn't that you *feel* guilty but that you *are* guilty. But the gospel of Jesus Christ has a permanent solution to your pain: the blood of Jesus Christ brings complete and eternal forgiveness! Your conscience can be cleansed *forever*. Your heart can be set free from condemnation, *forever*. Your emotions need not be damaged by self-contempt but can be redeemed and renewed and enjoyed, *forever*."

I say this to you because of what the author of Hebrews says that God says. Here it is for us to see and read and hear and behold: God promises never ever to remember our sins or lawless deeds! Hebrews 10:17 is one of the most glorious declarations in all of Scripture, and I want you to hear it with a force and energy you've never experienced before. I want you to hear it in a way that actually changes your life and your relationship with God.

Our focus, therefore, is this one verse. But as you well know, no text like this hangs isolated in the Bible. It does not exist in a vacuum. It is always nestled in, as it were, among other statements that supply us with a context or framework for understanding it. That context is the nine chapters of Hebrews that precede.

Jesus Is Better!

The theme of Hebrews is simple: *Jesus is better!* Jesus—who he is, what he has done, and what he is doing now at the right hand of the Father in heaven—is infinitely superior to and greater and more glorious than everything that preceded him in the Old Testament. In fact, everything that preceded him in the Old Testament pointed forward to his coming. The various symbols and shadows and Levitical code sacrifices of the Old Testament were designed to point forward to the coming of Jesus Christ.

If you haven't read Hebrews lately, let me take you on a brief, whirlwind tour of the book, at least up to chapter 10. We see in chapter 1 that Jesus is better than the *prophets* of the Old Testament. He is superior to the *angels* who fulfill God's bidding and do his will. We see in chapter 2 that the *salvation* he secures for us is superior to anything that the Old Testament law of Moses could provide. In chapter 3, we are told how Jesus is better than *Moses*. In chapter 4, we are told that the "rest" provided by Jesus is greater than the "rest" that came through *Joshua* and the promised land of Canaan. In chapters 5–7, our author explains in considerable detail how Jesus as high priest is better than *Aaron* and all the other high priests in the history of Israel. In chapter 8, he explains how the *new covenant* inaugurated by Jesus is superior in every way to the old covenant that came through Moses. And in chapter 9, we read that the sacrifice that Jesus offered of himself to deal with sin once and for all time is incomparably superior to the *sacrifices* of bulls and goats and lambs that were offered during the time of the Old Testament.

The book of Hebrews often stirs people to ask this question: If the blood of bulls and goats could never "take away" (10:4) the sins of the people of Israel, how were people in the time of the Old Testament saved? It wasn't by works. It wasn't through obedience to the law of Moses. It was by faith in that to which the sacrifices pointed. An Old Testament believer said, in effect, "I know the blood of bulls and goats cannot take away my sin. If it could, it wouldn't be shed in sacrifice year after year. The only thing that can take away my sin is that perfect sacrifice that God has promised he will provide in due course. I don't know fully what that will entail or look like. But my only hope for eternal life is to trust that what these animal sacrifices symbolize and typify and prophesy will one day be offered up on my behalf to atone finally and forever for my sins." That is how a person living during the time of the Old Testament was saved.

Hebrews 10:14 is a remarkable and extremely important passage: "For by a single offering he has perfected for all time those who are being sanctified." I want to draw your attention to something that most people ignore or fail to see. This is you, Christian. He's talking about you. And he says that Christ "has perfected (you) for all time." Don't overlook the past tense. Something has happened to you through faith in Jesus that is foundational to your Christian identity and life. You have been perfected! It is accomplished, finished, and complete, and nothing can add to it or detract from it.

This doesn't mean you will never again sin or make mistakes or forget where you left your car keys. It doesn't mean you will never lose your temper when someone cuts you off on the highway or you will never look upon someone with lust or envy those who have something you lack. Rather, the perfection that the author of Hebrews has in view is the forgiveness of sins. This is yet another reference to what I earlier described as your eternal union with Christ. You are *perfect* in the sense that God has forgiven all your sins and declared you righteous in his sight, and thus qualified you for acceptance in his presence. And that will never change. We'll see that more clearly when we look at verse 17.

So, how do we know that the perfection here in verse 14a is not sinless perfection, as if to suggest that when we believe in Jesus we cease forever to sin? We know it because of verse 14b, where we read that those who are "perfected" "*are being* sanctified." Notice the change in tense. We have been perfected in the past. It is accomplished and complete. But we are being sanctified in the present. If we are still in need of daily sanctification, we obviously are not yet free from sin.

This is more than a little shocking when you stop to think about it. Martin Luther, the great sixteenth-century Protestant Reformer, would often describe Christians with the Latin phrase, *simul iustus et peccator*: "simultaneously righteous/just and a sinner." We are those who have been "perfected" in that our sins are finally and forever forgiven; at the same time, we battle with sin and are gradually and progressively being made more and more like Jesus in our personal experience.

We now return to the one text that concerns us most: "I will remember their sins and their lawless deeds no more" (Heb. 10:17).

It's important for us to remember that God does in fact "remember" many things and we should be grateful for it. Frequently in the Old Testament, we are assured that God remembers his people, the promises he has given them, and especially the covenant that he has made with them (see Pss. 74:2; 105:8, 42; 106:45; 111:5). But when it comes to our sins, well, that's another matter!

You and I certainly remember our sins and evil deeds, all too often. We can't shake free from them. They nag at our hearts and haunt us and torment us and oppress our souls. There is a constant piercing of the conscience. And the only way to break free from that remembrance is to remind ourselves that God does not remember!

As I noted earlier, God doesn't gain knowledge. God doesn't lose knowledge. He neither learns nor forgets. He knows all things instantly and eternally, now and forever. So, when he says he won't remember our sins, he means, "I'll never bring it up and use it against you. I'll never take your sins into consideration when it comes to determining who is granted entrance into my eternal kingdom. I'll never appeal to your sins as grounds for condemning you."

There is obviously a difference in our experience between "forgetting" and "choosing not to remember." Forgetting is unavoidable. It happens by nature, not by choice. You can't choose to forget. It just happens. It doesn't require any effort to forget something. You get busy, distracted, tired, and things slip from your mind.

This is not what happens to God. God cannot forget in the literal sense of the term, and certainly not in the same way you and I do. God doesn't suffer from mental lapses. His mind is infinitely perfect and powerful. Rather, God willingly chooses not to remember. Thus, it isn't so much that the knowledge of our sins and lawless deeds has been erased from God's mind. Rather, God promises us that he will not remember our shortcomings and sin. He will not remind *himself* of our failures. And he will not remind *us* of them. They play no part in determining or shaping our eternal relationship with him. He will never throw them in our face or subtly drop hints about the ways we've failed.

"But wait a minute! Doesn't the Holy Spirit still convict us of sin and call us to confession and repentance?"

Yes, he certainly does. Although that may seem to conflict with Hebrews 10:17, it makes perfectly good sense when you keep in mind, once again, the vitally important distinction between our eternal union with Christ and our experiential communion with Christ that I mentioned in chapter 1.

Once again, our *eternal union* has to do with our salvation and our status in the sight of God. We are united by faith to Christ, and nothing can change or undermine that reality. This is what the author of Hebrews had in mind when he said that we have been "perfected for all time" (Heb. 10:14). And God's promise to us is that our eternal union with Christ will never be threatened or altered simply because we have a bad day that, in turn, causes God to have a bad day such that he decides to "remember" our sins. That will never, ever happen.

But our experiential communion with Christ is something that can change from day to day. Our *enjoyment* of that eternal union and the *peace* in our hearts that flows from it can fluctuate depending on our obedience. I am always and forever united to Christ by faith, but I don't always feel it or enjoy it or experience it from one day to the next. Disobedience and sin can greatly affect my communion with Christ but never my union with him.

Our fear is that when we fail and sin, God will say, "Ah hah! Gotcha! I remember now when you did this before. I gave you a free pass. I gave you a second chance. And there you go again. You're such a disappointment!" No! Never!

So I ask you: What would your Christian life look like if you woke up each day, went about your tasks and responsibilities, and fell asleep each night with the unassailable confidence in your heart that God will never remember your sins and lawless deeds? To know without hesitation or qualification or the slightest doubt that when God looks at you and thinks about you and hears your prayers that he refuses to remember your sins or lawless deeds, not because there aren't any, not because you've been especially good this week, but solely because Jesus offered himself as a sacrifice in your place once and for all time—to know this and to experience the joy and power and peace it brings, is simply too marvelous for words.

Now, let me close with an appeal and an offer to you who do not yet know Christ as Lord and Savior. Do you agonize over your sin and lawless deeds? Do you live daily in distress and fear that God will reject and judge you, now and forever? Do you desire that God would never again remember your sins? That can happen today, right now, and it will last forever.

I offer you Jesus Christ. Or better still, Jesus offers himself to you, he who gave himself as a sacrifice for sinful men and women like us. Through that sacrifice, he has atoned for sin; he has satisfied the wrath and justice of God. And now all that is required is that you acknowledge your need of a savior and that you repent of those sins and lawless deeds and put your trust and hope and confidence in Jesus alone. The moment that happens, God says to you, "I will remember your sins and your lawless deeds *no more.*" And that means forever!

14

And Three Things He Doesn't and Never Will Do with Your Sin

WE'VE NEARLY COME TO the end of our journey through what Scripture tells us about God's response to our sin. Thus far, we've learned twelve things God has done:

He laid our sin on his Son, Jesus Christ.

He has forgiven us of our sin.

He has cleansed us from our sin.

He has covered our sin.

He has cast our sin behind his back.

He has removed our sin as far as the east is from the west.

He has passed over our sin.

He has trampled our sin underfoot.

He has cast our sin into the depths of the sea.

He has blotted out our sin.

He has turned his face away from our sin.

He has forgotten all our sin.

But above and beyond the dozen things God did with your sin, there are three things he doesn't and never will do. These three glorious truths are so intertwined and overlapping that I will examine them together. Two of them appear in the same verse. Once again, in Psalm 103:10, we are told that God "does not deal with us according to our sins, nor repay us according to our iniquities." And in Psalm 32:2, David declares that person blessed "against whom the LORD counts no iniquity."

God's Way of Dealing with Sin vs. Our Way

Consider for a moment how we "deal" with others. We keep fresh in our minds their injustices toward us. We nurture the memory of their faults and failings. We never let them forget what they did and we often make sure others are mindful of it as well. We seek every opportunity, often secretly and surreptitiously, to make them pay for their transgressions. We hold it in our hearts and over their heads and persuade ourselves that it's only fair that they be treated this way.

Our good and gracious God, on the other hand, "does *not* deal with us according to our sins" (Ps. 103:10). Our sins do not constitute the rule or standard or plumb line according to which God makes his decisions on how to treat us. He does not recall or bring to the fore or publicly announce our history of hatred and lust and blasphemy and greed and pride before he formulates his plan for our life or before responding to something we've just said or done.

When we interact one with another, all too often we let our response be guided or dictated by past infractions. It may have been a betrayal, perhaps in the form of baseless gossip where they slandered you in order to advance their own cause. Or maybe they failed to come through on something they promised you could always count on. Or someone may have broken your confidence and passed along information that they assured you they would never share. You may have been the victim of some injustice or abuse. In many cases, it turns out to be that a close friend whom you were certain would never leave you suddenly abandons you for reasons that have no basis.

I could go on and on about the ways in which we sin against each other. Some of the ways are more serious and severe than others, but they all hurt, to one degree or another. And the memory of these offenses lingers in our hearts and later fuels and gives shape to how we treat that person. We "deal" with them on the basis of these painful experiences. We respond to them in kind, having convinced ourselves that this is what justice would require.

The point of the psalmist is that this is precisely what God will never do. In responding to us this way, God is not ignoring our faults and failures. He is not winking at sin or pretending that it never happened. And it certainly isn't because he is more loving than just. As we'll see shortly, his guarantee that he will never "deal" with us according to our sins is rooted in something so profound and glorious that we often find it more than a little difficult to believe.

Better still is the second statement in Psalm 103:10, that God does not "repay us according to our iniquities." It's certainly not because our iniquities do not deserve repayment. They are deep and many and heinous and are deserving of the most severe, indeed, eternal judgment. But those who "fear him" (v. 11) need never fear that he will exact payment or demand suffering or insist, according to the rigors of his law and unyielding holiness, that we endure the penal consequences of violating his will and ways.

Most of us, sad to confess, have developed all sorts of devious ways of repaying those who have hurt us. We might choose simply to ignore the offender, treating them as if they are now unimportant to us or, worse still, dangerous and to be avoided. We pay back those who intentionally sinned against us by withholding forgiveness and making sure that others are fully aware of everything they've done. A clever bumper sticker says it well: "Don't get mad. Get even!" Revenge has become something of a pastime in our culture, a relational hobby of sorts.

But not with God. I've been in almost daily dialogue via email with a young man I've never met who lives in perpetual, incessant fear that God is going to pull the rug out from under his salvation. He is possessed of what can only be described as an overly sensitive conscience. Assurance of salvation, if he ever experiences it at all, is grounded in his ability to consistently avoid sin in all its many forms. Needless to say, I'm not suggesting that any decision on his part to live in unrepentant disobedience is of no consequence. I've told him on numerous occasions that willful, unrepentant, defiant disobedience is often an indication that one's purported profession of faith in Christ is spurious and superficial. But his life is dominated by an obsessive concern that one day God will "repay" him for all his failures and that all hope of salvation will be lost. His compulsive introspective approach to Christian living has undermined his ability to look away from himself to the righteousness of Jesus as his only hope. I have directed him to Psalm 103:8–14 and other related texts, but to no avail, at least at the time of my writing this book.

Similarly, I have directed his attention to David's wonderful declaration that we need never fear that God will impute to us or count against us the many sins we have committed (32:2). What is the meaning behind such words as "count" or "reckon" or "impute"? The idea is that God is not keeping a written record of our transgressions to make use of them as grounds for our condemna-tion. He will never bring into the courtroom a ledger in which is recorded the many spiritual debts we have failed to pay or the moral offenses we have committed, all with a view to securing a guilty verdict from the Judge.

But this doesn't mean that God never "counts" or "records" anything at all. In yet another psalm, David finds solace in the fact that God has "kept count" of his "tossings" or wanderings. "Put my tears in your bottle," he prays. "Are they not in your book?" (56:8). David wants there to be a permanent record of his sufferings and lamenting. In other words, David "imagines the existence of record books at the heavenly court analogous to those at an earthly court and asks God to make sure that these include 'my lamentations,' more literally the visible shaking or tossing that were the outward expression of anguish."[1] David does not envision his "tears" as establishing some form of merit or credit with God, but "they appeal to God's compassion and therefore push God to take action against the attackers."[2]

So, yes, God does *count* certain aspects of our experience. He does indeed keep a record and often appeals to such when he turns to act on our behalf. But it is a record of our suffering, our tears, and our lamentation. He has promised never to keep record of our sins. The latter, praise God, are erased or blotted out from his book (see chapter 12).

It's entirely possible that some reading this will draw the wrong conclusion. They will conclude that I'm saying our sins have no effect in any sense of the term on our relationship with God. They

1 John Goldingay, *Psalms*, vol. 2, *Psalms 42–89* (Grand Rapids, MI: Baker Academic, 2007), 187.
2 Goldingay, *Psalms*, vol. 2, 187.

will assume that what I'm suggesting is that we can continue to live in complete joy and peace and intimacy with the Lord no matter what we do or fail to do. Nothing could be further from the truth.

Once again, we have to keep fresh in our thinking the difference between our eternal union with God and our experiential communion with him. When the psalmist boldly declares that God does not "deal" with us according to our sin and will never "repay" us according to our iniquities and declines to "count" or impute our sins to us, he is talking about our eternal union. In that relationship with God, we stand secure and safe because of his commitment to preserve and protect us. But when it comes to our daily, experiential capacity to enjoy the truth of our eternal union and to relish the peace that surpasses all understanding and to feel the joy in our hearts of being a child of God, repeated and unrepentant sin most assuredly does come into play. It clouds our minds and hinders our hearts from feeling God's affection for us. We cannot presume that God will hear our prayers while we cling tenaciously so some sinful or addictive habit. So, yes, there is damage done to our sensible enjoyment of all that God is for us in Jesus. But when it comes to our salvation and eternal relationship with the Lord, we can rejoice in knowing that Psalm 103:8–14 is ever and always true.

Now, here's the question: *Why* does God *not* deal with us according to our sins? *Why* does he *not* repay us according to our iniquities? *Why* does he *not* count or reckon our sins against us? In other words, on what grounds does he take such magnanimous and marvelous action? Does he simply wave his hand of mercy and dismiss our guilt? Does he merely shrug off our rebellion and unbelief and hostility as if they were nothing and of no consequence? Does he ignore the dictates of his holiness when he forgives us? Does he pretend that justice matters little or that love trumps righteousness?

Clearly, the answer is no! We have seen the explanation for this repeatedly since the start of this book, but it can't hurt to say it again and again. The reason God does not deal with *us* according to our sins is because he has dealt with *Jesus* in accordance with what our sins require! The reason why God does not repay *us* according to our iniquities is because he has repaid his *Son* in accordance with what holiness demands—in perfect harmony, I must add, with the will and voluntary love of the Son himself!

David wrote these words of hope and life in Psalm 103 from within the context of the Old Testament sacrificial system. He could confidently speak of such grace and kindness because he personally knew of the Day of Atonement, of the blood sacrifice, of the scapegoat onto whose head his sins were symbolically placed and transferred (see Lev. 16).

In our case, on this side of the cross that forever and finally fulfills these old covenant types and symbols, we can confidently rest in the freedom of forgiveness because God has "put forward [Christ Jesus] as a propitiation by his blood" (Rom. 3:25). God did not willy-nilly cast aside our sins as if they did not matter. Rather, he "laid on him [the Son, our Savior] the iniquity of us all" (Isa. 53:6). God did not casually ignore the dictates of his holy and righteous character. Rather, he "pierced" Jesus "for our transgressions" and "crushed" him "for our iniquities" (v. 5).

This, and this alone, is why we can sing and celebrate that God does not and never will "deal with us according to our sins" or "repay us according to our iniquities." The measure of God's "steadfast love" (Ps. 103:11) is the depth of the sacrifice he endured in giving up his only Son to suffer in our stead (see Rom. 8:32).

I hope you can see why the current debate over penal substitutionary atonement is so eternally important, for if God did *not* deal with the Lord Jesus Christ according to your sins, he will deal with *you* in accordance with them. And if God did *not* repay in his Son what your iniquities deserve, he will repay *you*. It's just that simple.

Psalm 103 begins with the exhortation that we not forget all the many benefits that God has graciously bestowed, chief among which is that he "forgives all your iniquity" (v. 3). Now we know how. Now we know why. So let us all sing:

Before the throne of God above
I have a strong and perfect plea.
A great High Priest whose Name is Love
Who ever lives and pleads for me.

My name is graven on His hands,
My name is written on His heart.
I know that while in Heaven He stands,
No tongue can bid me thence depart.

When Satan tempts me to despair
And tells me of the guilt within,
Upward I look and see Him there
Who made an end of all my sin.

Because the sinless Savior died
My sinful soul is counted free.
For God the just is satisfied
To look on Him and pardon me.

Behold Him there the risen Lamb,
My perfect spotless righteousness,
The great unchangeable I AM,
The King of glory and of grace.

One in Himself I cannot die,
My soul is purchased by His blood!
My life is hid with Christ on high,
With Christ, my Savior and my God!
    (C. L. Bancroft, 1863; emphasis added)

15

The Gospel

THERE IS A SENSE in which this entire book is an elaborate unpacking of what we mean when we use the word *gospel*.[1] In other
words, the gospel is what God, through the person and work of
Jesus Christ, has done with our sin. Of course, everyone who is a
Christian *ought* to know what the gospel is. But we can no longer
assume they do. Times are changing, and in many ways, for the
worse. We are in an odd season when the very foundations of the
Christian faith are being challenged and reconfigured. As much
as we might like to think that everyone knows what the gospel is,
they don't. And many of those who think they do have actually
embraced a concept of the gospel that is shaped and governed
more by the culture or the political climate than it is by the word
of God. Therefore, we would do well to conclude this book with
a summation of its most salient points.

We should begin with a brief mention of several texts that highlight how important the gospel is. If any are inclined to think of it

---

1   In this chapter, I have made extensive use of my article "The Gospel" that was first published
    in the *ESV Systematic Theology Study Bible* (Wheaton, IL: Crossway, 2017).

as a secondary issue or one that doesn't call for careful definition, these passages of Scripture will set the record straight:

> "For whoever would save his life will lose it, but whoever loses his life for my sake and the gospel's will save it." (Mark 8:35)

> Jesus said, "Truly, I say to you, there is no one who has left house or brothers or sisters or mother or father or children or lands, for my sake and for the gospel, who will not receive a hundredfold now in this time, houses and brothers and sisters and mothers and children and lands, with persecutions, and in the age to come eternal life." (10:29–30)

> "But I do not account my life of any value nor as precious to myself, if only I may finish my course and the ministry that I received from the Lord Jesus, to testify to the gospel of the grace of God." (Acts 20:24)

> I am astonished that you are so quickly deserting him who called you in the grace of Christ and are turning to a different gospel—not that there is another one, but there are some who trouble you and want to distort the gospel of Christ. But even if we or an angel from heaven should preach to you a gospel contrary to the one we preached to you, let him be accursed. As we have said before, so now I say again: If anyone is preaching to you a gospel contrary to the one you received, let him be accursed. (Gal. 1:6–9)

> In him you also, when you heard the word of truth, the gospel of your salvation, and believed in him, were sealed with the promised Holy Spirit. (Eph. 1:13)[2]

---

2 See also Col. 1:23; 1 Thess. 2:4; 2 Tim. 1:8; Phil. 1:27, to name a few.

This "gospel," then, is the gloriously great good news of what our triune God has graciously done in the incarnation, life, death, and resurrection of Jesus Christ to satisfy his own wrath against us and to secure the forgiveness of sins and perfect righteousness for all who trust in him by faith alone. Christ fulfilled, on our behalf, the perfectly obedient life under God's law that we should have lived but never could. He died, in our place, the death that we deserved to suffer but now never will. And by his rising from the dead, he secured for those who believe the promise of a resurrected and glorified life in a new heaven and a new earth in fellowship with the Father, Son, and Holy Spirit forever.

The gospel is fundamentally about something that *has* happened. It is an accomplished event, an unalterable fact of history. Nothing can undo the gospel. No power in heaven or earth can overturn or reverse it. But as a settled achievement it also exerts a radical and far-reaching influence into both our present experience and our future hopes. Central to why it is the "best" news imaginable is that the glory of what God has already done in and through Jesus transforms everything now and yet to come.

This gospel is not only the means by which people have been saved, but also the truth and power by which people are being sanctified (1 Cor. 15:1–2). It is the truth of the gospel that enables us to genuinely and joyfully do what is pleasing to God and to grow in progressive conformity to the image of Christ. Thus, we must never think that the gospel is solely for unbelievers. It is for Christians, at every stage of their lives. There is nothing in the Christian life that is "post" gospel!

It would not be an exaggeration to say that the gospel is the gravitational center of both our individual experience and the shape of local church life. We see this in numerous biblical texts.

For example, the gospel is Christocentric: it is about Jesus, God's son (Mark 1:1; Rom. 1:9). Both Mark (Mark 1:14) and Paul (Rom. 1:1; 1 Thess. 2:2) describe it as the gospel "of God," insofar as he is its source and the cause of all that it entails. Humans do not create or craft the gospel: they respond to it by repenting of their sins and believing its message (Mark 1:15) concerning what God has done in the life, death, and resurrection of Jesus.

The gospel, then, is "the word of truth" that proclaims our "salvation" (Eph. 1:13). It is marked by grace (Acts 20:24), which is to say it is the message of God's gracious provision, apart from human works, of all that is necessary to reconcile us to himself both now and for eternity. Indeed, the gospel is the foundation, pattern, and power for how we respond to unjust suffering (1 Pet. 2:18–25; 3:17–18), the way we relate to our spouse (Eph. 5:25–33), how we use our money (2 Cor. 8:8–9; 9:13), the manner in which we forgive those who've sinned against us (Eph. 4:32; Col. 3:13), and the zeal with which we serve others (Mark 10:43–45; 1 John 3:16–18). This good news of what God has done in and through Christ's death (1 Cor. 2:2) and resurrection (2 Tim. 2:8) brings peace (Eph. 6:15), life, and immortality (2 Tim. 1:10) to those who receive it.

These truths are of paramount and eternal importance, for to "distort the gospel of Christ" (Gal. 1:7) or to preach one that is "different" from or "contrary" to what the apostles made known is to come under a divine curse (vv. 6, 8–9).

So, how does the gospel change us? Of what practical, daily importance is it? I believe it was Tim Keller who first directed my attention to a helpful distinction that will help us answer this question. He pointed to the sad fact that Christians often live in an "if/then" relationship with God. *If* I do what is right, *then* God will love me. *If* I give more money to missions, *then* God will provide me with a raise at work. *If* I avoid sinful habits, *then* I will be spared suffering and humiliation. It's a *conditional* relationship that is based on the principle of *merit*.

But the gospel calls us to live in a "because/therefore" relationship with the Lord. *Because* we have been justified by faith in Christ, *therefore* we have peace with God (Rom. 5:1). *Because* Christ died for us, *therefore* we are forgiven. *Because* Christ has fulfilled the law in our place, *therefore* we are set free from its demands and penalty. This is an *unconditional* relationship that is based on the principle of *grace*.

When our approach to Christian living is based on the "if/then" paradigm, we will find ourselves immersed in the religious life in which our acceptance is based on obedience. Our motivation is fear and insecurity. Our identity and self-worth are dependent on what we do and how well we do it. When we fail, we're worthless. When we succeed, we're valuable. But in the gospel-centered life, acceptance is based on grace and the mercy of God. Our motivation is joy and faith in the promise of yet more grace in the future. Our identity and self-worth are dependent on who God has made us to be in his image and who he is transforming us to be through the power of the Spirit. When we fail, he still loves us. When we succeed, our success redounds to his praise and honor.

Five Foundational Truths of the Gospel

With that in mind, we must also keep our focus on the following five foundational truths that make the gospel not just good news but the very best news.

First, the gospel is rooted in the call of Israel and is consummated in the Messiah, Jesus of Nazareth, who is the fulfillment of the types and shadows of the old covenant. As such, the gospel must never be thought of as an abstract, ahistorical idea, as if it were disconnected from or unrelated to the concrete realities of life on earth. The life, death, and resurrection of Jesus are thus to be seen as the pivotal chapter in the unfolding story of God's redemptive purpose for humanity.

Second, the gospel is not something that God requires. The gospel is what God provides. There is of course, an intrinsic demand built into the gospel. The good news that is proclaimed calls for a response of faith and repentance. But our faith and repentance are not themselves the gospel. Our personal testimony is not the gospel. We cannot *be* the gospel, but we do *bear witness* to it.

Third, the gospel is not a command or an imperative, demanding things you must do. The gospel is a statement of accomplished fact, an indicative, declaring things God has already done. Again, of course, we do things because of the gospel. But our doing things isn't itself the gospel.

Fourth, the gospel is not about human action. The gospel is about divine achievement. Put another way, the gospel is about God's provision, not man's response. The gospel is not a moralistic *Do!* The gospel is a merciful *Done!* There are undoubtedly multiple consequences of the gospel that extend beyond its impact on the individual and his relationship to God. The gospel invariably issues a call for human action. Among the implications or results of the gospel are the cultivation of humility (Phil. 2:1–5), the pursuit of racial reconciliation (Eph. 2:11–22) and social justice (Philem. 8–20), a commitment to harmony and peace among men (Rom. 15:5–7; Heb. 12:14), and the demonstration of love one for another (1 John 3:16, 23). But we must never confuse the content of the gospel with its consequences. There is a vitally important distinction between the essence of the gospel and its entailments, between its content and its consequences.

Fifth, whereas the gospel is God's redeeming act in Jesus on behalf of sinful men and women, we must not overlook the fact that it is only because of the gospel that we have a sure and certain hope for cosmic transformation. The good news of God's saving act in Christ is thus the foundation for our confidence in the ultimate triumph of God's kingdom (1 Cor. 15:20–24), the end of physical death (1 Cor. 15:25–26; Rev. 21:4), the defeat of Satan (John 16:11; Col. 2:13–15; Heb. 2:14; 1 John 3:8), the eradication of all evil (Rev. 21:4, 8), and the removal of the curse that rests on our physical environment and, in turn, the consummation of God's purpose for all creation in the new heavens and new earth (Rom. 8:18–25).

Thinking of the gospel in these terms helps explain what we see in Acts 20:24. There Paul writes, "But I do not account my life of any value nor as precious to myself, if only I may finish my course and the ministry that I received from the Lord Jesus, to testify to the gospel of the grace of God." How do we account for this kind of zeal, this depth of devotion? Perhaps the answer is found in something Paul said later in Acts 20 regarding God's gracious work for us in Christ Jesus. In Acts 20:28, as part of his exhortation to the elders in the church at Ephesus, Paul said this: "Pay careful attention to yourselves and to all the flock, in which the Holy Spirit has made you overseers, to care for the church of God, which he obtained with his own blood."

It strikes many as odd for Paul to speak of "God" the Father obtaining the church with "his own blood," and rightly so, as the Father did not become incarnate and die on a cross. The Father did not bleed. The Son did. Thus, a few manuscripts read, "to care for the church of the *Lord* which he obtained with his own blood," the reference being to Jesus himself rather than to God the Father. But "the church of God" is almost certainly the superior reading and thus has in view the Father, not the Son. But if so, how can it be said that God the Father obtained the church with "his own blood"?

The best rendering of this statement is this: "the church of God, which he obtained with the blood of his own." The words rendered "his own" would then be a reference to Jesus—such as we find in Romans 8:32—designed to focus on the intimacy that characterizes the love between them. "His own" is the translation of a single word in the Greek text and is likely a term of endearment, portraying a close family relationship, thereby pointing to the affection and love of the Father for the Son. Hence, God the Father bought the church with the blood of "his own" dear Son, Jesus. This is the gospel! This is the good news we proclaim, that God has purchased or redeemed a community of scurrilous sinners by offering up as a ransom for their souls the precious blood of "his own" dear and greatly loved Son!

The Gospel Affects All of Life

Earlier I mentioned a number of ways that the gospel influences virtually all our relationships and responsibilities in life and ministry. Let's slow down a bit and unpack these in more detail.

Our approach to suffering—that is, how to suffer unjustly without growing bitter and resentful—is tied directly to the way Christ suffered for us and did so without reviling those who reviled him: "when he suffered, he did not threaten, but continued entrusting himself to him who judges justly" (1 Pet. 2:23; cf. 2:18–25; 3:17–18).

Or take humility as another example. The basis for Paul's appeal that we "do nothing from selfish ambition or conceit, but in humility count others more significant than" ourselves is the self-sacrifice of God the Son in becoming a human and submitting to death, even death on a cross (Phil. 2:1–5 in relation to 2:6–11). And as husbands, we are to love our wives "as Christ loved the church and gave himself up for her" (Eph. 5:25; see further vv. 26–33).

Why should we be generous and sacrificial with our money? Because, says Paul, "you know the grace of our Lord Jesus Christ, that though he was rich, yet for your sake he became poor, so that you by his poverty might become rich" (2 Cor. 8:9; cf. 9:13). Likewise, we are to forgive one another "as God in Christ forgave" us (Eph. 4:32; cf. Col. 3:13). We are to "walk in love" toward each other, says Paul, "as Christ loved us and gave himself up for us" (Eph. 5:1–2). We are to serve one another in humility as Christ served his disciples by washing their feet and eventually suffering in their stead (John 13:1–20).

The freedom we have in Christ, says Paul in Romans 14, is to be controlled in its exercise by the recognition that the weaker brother who might be damaged by our behavior is one for whom Christ died. Paul encourages us to pray for all based on the fact that Christ "gave himself as a ransom for all" (1 Tim. 2:1–7)

If that were not enough, countless passages in the New Testament direct us back to the reality of the gospel and what Christ has done for us through it as the primary way to combat those false beliefs and feelings that hinder our spiritual growth. So, for example,

When you don't feel loved by others, meditate on Romans 5:5–11 and 8:35–39.
When you don't have a sense of any personal value, read Matthew 10:29–31 and 1 John 3:1–3.

When you struggle to find meaning in life, study Ephesians 1:4–14 and Romans 11:33–36.

When you don't feel useful, consider 1 Corinthians 12:7–27 and 15:58.

When you feel unjustly criticized, rest in the truth of Romans 8:33–34.

When you feel excluded by others, rejoice in Hebrews 13:5–6.

When you feel you have no good works, let Ephesians 2:8–10 have its effect.

When you are constantly asking, "Who am I?" take courage in 1 Peter 2:9–10.

When you live in fear that other people have the power to destroy or undermine who you are, be strengthened by Romans 8:31–34 and Hebrews 13:5–6.

When you don't feel like you belong anywhere, take comfort from 1 Corinthians 12:13 and Ephesians 4:1–16.

When Satan accuses you of being a constant failure, remind him and yourself of 1 Corinthians 1:30–31.

When Satan tells you that you are an embarrassment to the church, quote Ephesians 3:10.

When you find yourself bitter towards the church and indifferent regarding its ministries, reflect on Acts 20:28.

When you find yourself shamed into silence when confronted by non-Christians, be encouraged with 2 Timothy 1:8–12.

When you find yourself experiencing prejudice against those of another race or culture, memorize and act upon the truth of Romans 1:16; 2 Corinthians 5:14–16; Ephesians 2:11–22; and Revelation 5.

When you struggle with pride and boasting in your own achievements, be humbled by Romans 3:27–28 and 1 Corinthians 1:18–31.

When you feel despair and hopelessness, let Romans 5:1–10 restore your confidence.

When you feel defeated by sin and hopeless ever to change, delight yourself in Romans 7:24–25.

When you feel condemned by God for your multiple, repeated failures, speak aloud the words of Romans 8:1.

When you lack power to resist conforming to the world, consider Romans 12:1–2 and Galatians 6:14.

When you feel weak and powerless, be energized by Romans 16:25.

When you are tempted sexually, never forget 1 Corinthians 6:18–20.

And again, when you find yourself saying,

"I'm not having any impact in life or on others," be uplifted by 2 Corinthians 12:9–10.

"I feel guilty and filled with shame all the time for my sins," be reminded of Ephesians 1:7.

"I live in constant fear," be encouraged by Luke 12:32 and Revelation 2:9–11.

"I struggle with anxiety and worry about everything," don't neglect the truth of Matthew 6:25–34; Philippians 4:6–7; and 1 Peter 5:6–7.

"I am defined and controlled by my past," look to 2 Corinthians 5:17.

"I live in fear that God will abandon me," consider his promise in Romans 8:35–38.

"I can't break free of my sins and bad habits," linger long with Romans 6:6, 14.

"I'm afraid to pray and fear that God will mock my petitions," take heart from Hebrews 4:14–16.

"I carry grudges against those who've wronged me and live in bitterness towards them," reflect and meditate on Colossians 3:12–13.

"I can't find strength to serve others, fearing that I'll be taken advantage of by them," let Mark 10:45 and Philippians 2:5–11 have their way in your life.

"I'm a spiritual orphan and belong to no one," rejoice in Galatians 4:4–7.

Each of these texts refers to the gospel of what God has done for us in the life, death, and resurrection of Christ, and each text applies that gospel truth to the particular problem noted. These, then, are just a handful of the ways that the gospel affects all of life, all of ministry, and everything we seek to be and do and accomplish as Christians and as local churches.

The Morphing and Muting of the Gospel

I'm not an alarmist by nature. I'm inclined to dismiss those who cry wolf or tell us that the sky is falling, and I'm especially impatient with last-days fanaticism that insists the second coming of Christ is just around the corner—although, in the case of this latter prediction, I hope and pray they are right! But I am alarmed and greatly concerned by something in our day and I am quite fanatical about alerting the body of Christ to what is happening. I'm talking about what has often been described as the *morphing* and *muting* of the gospel. By the "morphing" of the gospel, I simply mean the many ways in which it is being redefined and recast in a way, so we are told, that is more compatible with the postmodern world in which we live. By the "muting" of the gospel, I simply mean the tragic silence when it comes to proclaiming the gospel to a lost and dying world.

Let me focus here on a couple of ways in which the gospel is morphing in our day. I have in mind the tendency either to *shrink* the gospel or to *expand* it, both of which, by the way, are typically done in reaction to the other. Often people are tempted to shrink the gospel by paring off its rough and potentially offensive edges, thereby adapting it to the particular cultural context in which they live and minister. I'm all for contextualization. In fact, it's largely unavoidable. But this does not require that the gospel itself be reconfigured or redefined so radically that it ceases to be concerned with the redemptive and saving activity of God in Christ.

On the other hand, many do damage to the gospel by *expanding* it to encompass virtually everything. In other words, if we make the gospel mean everything, it ends up meaning nothing. If the gospel means everything, one can no longer differentiate it from its counterfeits. We must distinguish between what the gospel is and what its inevitable or intended consequences are. For example, the gospel *is* the work of Christ in reconciling us to God, but the intended consequence is that we also are to be reconciled to one another. The gospel *is* redemption of body, soul, and spirit through faith in Jesus, but the intended consequence is that this redemption extends to the natural creation and the deliverance of creation from the curse. The gospel *is* justification by faith alone in Christ alone, but the intended consequence is that it leads to the alleviation of poverty and suffering and homelessness.

Loving God with all my heart, soul, and mind, and my neighbor as myself is of critical importance: but that isn't the gospel. Taking note of Martin Luther King Jr. Day each year and being both aware of and actively engaged in the pursuit of civil rights is essential for all Christians: but that is not the gospel. Acknowledging Right to Life Sunday and actively working on behalf of the unborn is crucial: but it is not the gospel. Sharing your personal testimony of a radically changed life is something all of us should do: but that is not the gospel. In other words, the gospel must not be confused with what it produces. The content of the gospel is one thing; its consequences are another. As noted earlier, there is a difference between essence and entailment.

My point is that the gospel is not moral behavior; the gospel is not social action; the gospel is not raising money to fight the spread of AIDS in Africa; the gospel is not care for creation, interpersonal reconciliation, good deeds, feeding the hungry, clothing the naked, or housing the homeless. All these are of crucial importance, and Christian men and women should be encouraged to give of their time and money and energy to support these activities. Please do not think that by listing them in this way that I'm minimizing their value. But these activities are not the gospel. The gospel is God's activity, not ours. The gospel is his action, his work in and through the life, death, and resurrection of Jesus Christ to secure the forgiveness of sins of those who repent and trust in what he has done.

We celebrate and proclaim and protect this gospel because the gospel can accomplish what an Ivy League education cannot. Yes, I believe every person, as much as is humanly and financially possible, should pursue as much education as they reasonably can. Ignorance never yet greatly served the mission of the church. Education broadens the mind, enlightens the understanding, and captivates the imagination, but it is powerless to convert the soul and renew the spirit and fill the heart with joy in Jesus!

The gospel can accomplish what science cannot. Yes, science can improve the quality of our lives on earth, protect us from infectious diseases, and create devices that improve our communication. But it cannot redeem us from sin, impart forgiveness, or give us hope in the face of death. The gospel can accomplish what technology cannot. I'm grateful for technology, for the airline industry that enables me to travel, for the laptop computer on which I do my work and write my books, for the heating systems that keep us warm and the air conditioning systems that keep us cool. But technology cannot regenerate our hearts or bring us into the true knowledge of God. Praise God for nuclear energy and economic development and the entertainment industry and athletics and the international banking system. But for all their good, they cannot do what only the gospel can. They cannot give us God.

But the gospel can![3]

---

3 Among the many excellent resources on the gospel, I highly recommend John Piper, *God Is the Gospel: Meditations on God's Love as the Gift of Himself* (Wheaton, IL: Crossway, 2005); Greg Gilbert, *What Is the Gospel?* (Wheaton, IL: Crossway, 2010); Ray Ortlund, *The Gospel: How the Church Portrays the Beauty of Christ* (Wheaton, IL: Crossway, 2014); Gilbert, "A T4G 2020 Sermon: What Is and Isn't the Gospel?" 9Marks, April 15, 2020, https://www.9marks.org/; Kevin DeYoung and Greg Gilbert, *What Is the Mission of the Church? Making Sense of Social Justice, Shalom, and the Great Commission* (Wheaton, IL: Crossway, 2011); D. A. Carson, "What Is the Gospel?—Revisited," in *For the Fame of God's Name: Essays in Honor of John Piper*, ed. Sam Storms and Justin Taylor (Wheaton, IL: Crossway, 2010), 147–70.

16

"Uttermost" and "Always"!

IF OUR SINS ARE TRULY trampled underfoot, cast into the depths of the sea, and utterly blotted out of sight, never to rise up with shouts of condemnation, it is only because of what Jesus has done to secure our salvation. But we must never forget that the saving and preserving work of Christ on our behalf did not end with the cross and the empty tomb. Jesus was exalted to the right hand of the Father and there defends us and serves as our "advocate" (1 John 2:1) and intercessor (Rom. 8:34).

But wouldn't this suggest that the cross was left incomplete or unfinished? No, not at all. Dane Ortlund has answered this concern:

> The answer is that intercession applies what the atonement accomplished. Christ's present heavenly intercession on our behalf is a reflection of the fullness and victory and completeness of his earthly work, not a reflection of anything lacking in his earthly work. The atonement accomplished our salvation; intercession is the moment-by-moment application of that atoning work. In the past, Jesus did what he now talks about; in the present,

Jesus talks about what he then did. This is why the New Testament weds justification and intercession, such as in Romans 8:33–34: "Who shall bring any charge against God's elect? It is God who justifies. Who is to condemn? Christ Jesus is the one who died—more than that, who was raised—who is at the right hand of God, who indeed is interceding for us." Intercession is the constant hitting "refresh" of our justification in the court of heaven.[1]

Perhaps the most reassuring affirmation of this truth is found once again in the book of Hebrews, where the author reminds us that Jesus "is able to save to the uttermost those who draw near to God through him, since he always lives to make intercession for them" (7:25). And it is with that marvelous passage that I want to bring this book to a close.

No matter how seemingly helpful the many psychological formulas that enable us to cope with life may be, no matter how transforming the practical counsel we might find in today's world to help us with our problems may be, everything is either partial or periodic. They go only so far and for so long before they lose their capacity to make a difference.

Every person, every strategy, and every promise that comes our way will eventually fail us. If it's a friend, the day will come when they won't show up when we need them most. If it's a formula, the day will come when it proves inadequate to meet our need or answer our question or soothe our conscience or get us over the hurdle of some obstacle in life. Everything in life ultimately fails. Everyone in life ultimately falters. This isn't rank pessimism or

---

1   Dane Ortlund, "6 Qeustions about Christ's Heart for Sinners," Crossway (website), May 2, 2020, https://www.crossway.org/.

cynicism. This is realism. But there's no reason why this should be discouraging, for Jesus "is able to save to the uttermost those who draw near to God through him, since he always lives to make intercession for them."

"Uttermost" and "always." These two words are lifesaving. These two words are hope-giving. These two words are joy-awakening, heart-thrilling, and breathtaking in their force and implication. Many of you have tattoos. I do not. But if I were to get a tattoo, I know exactly what it would be. There would actually be two of them. On my right forearm would be the word "uttermost" and on the left "always"! Don't expect to see this happen anytime soon, but I can't think of anything more glorious to be reminded of on a daily basis than the truth embodied and expressed in these two wonderful words.

The word "uttermost" is probably qualitative in force. It means to the utmost degree. It means that nothing in the salvation Christ provides is lacking in any way. It means that there is nothing defective in what Christ has done or in the reconciliation with God that he has obtained for us. It means that this salvation is complete and whole and pervasive and all-encompassing.

We struggle to believe this because we think that surely somewhere there must be someone who is simply too sinful to be saved. And maybe that someone is me! Surely somewhere there is an individual whose failures are simply too many for Christ to save. Their shortcomings are too frequent for Christ to forgive. Their sins are too severe, too hard-hearted for Christ to redeem. Maybe the selfishness of some is too deep-seated for the salvation Christ offers to overcome. Maybe the guilt people feel is too deeply entrenched in their souls that no salvation, not even that offered by Jesus Christ, can cleanse and wipe clean.

That's how most of us at one time or another tend to think. Indeed, that's why I wrote this book. All too many are convinced that the quality and extent and frequency and selfishness and repetitive occurrence of our sins in life are greater than the quality and capacity of Christ's person and work to overcome. After all, there have to be limits to what even Jesus can do. There has to be a point beyond which he cannot and will not go. I mean, no one is *that* patient or kind or pure or loving. No one is *that* good or gracious or tender or longsuffering. At least that's how we tend to think.

Most of us at some time or another in life reach a point of complete frustration with ourselves. We're fed up with our failures and we're convinced that God is too. We envision God looking up as we run to him for the umpteenth time, saying, "Oh, no. Not *you* again! Enough already! I've had it up to here with your stupidity and your sin and how you always expect me to be there waiting for you with open arms, ready to start all over again. Well, that ends today. This simply can't go on forever." And it makes sense to us that he would react that way. As far as our own experience is concerned, we've learned that everything has a limit, a boundary, a point beyond which not even God can go.

But the point here in Hebrews 7:25 is that our thinking is bad and off base and skewed. The point of verse 25 is that we have sold God short. We have horribly misjudged what he's like and have terribly underestimated what he has done and will continue to do. That's the point of the word "uttermost"! This word is saying that there are no lengths to which God in Christ won't go to save you, that there are no sins you've committed, are committing, or will in the future commit that are beyond the power of Christ's atoning death to forgive. This word is saying that Jesus Christ has accomplished for you what no one else ever has, can, or will. He has left nothing undone. He has not failed to make provision for every need.

When you begin to think that God missed a step, I remind you that he saves to the "uttermost." When you begin to wonder whether there are limits to his love, I remind you that he saves to the "uttermost." When you struggle to believe that an infinitely holy and righteous God would ever allow someone as vile and sinful and wretched as you and me into his presence, I remind you that he saves to the "uttermost." And when you simply throw up your hands in frustration and confusion, declaring that nothing *this* good could possibly be literally true, I remind you that he saves to the "uttermost."

Jesus Christ not only saves to the uttermost, but he also *always* lives to make intercession for you. If the word "uttermost" has a *qualitative* force to it, "always" has a *quantitative* force. Or perhaps we should say a *temporal* force. It speaks of duration and extension in time. It means never-ending, never-ceasing. It points to something that is incessant, eternal, everlasting. It may actually be the case that we struggle more to understand the implications of the word "always" than we do the implications of the word "uttermost." The reason is that even if something given to us is perfect, that doesn't necessarily mean it will last forever. Nothing lasts forever. Or does it?

It seems that everything we experience has a *shelf life* or an *expiration date*. "Good until July 14, 2022," it says on the medicine bottle. Change your oil every five thousand miles. Replace the filter on your air conditioning unit every six months. Be sure you install fresh batteries at least once a year in your smoke alarm in the house. "I take you to be my lawfully wedded wife/husband until death do us part." So not even marriage lasts forever. Nothing lasts. Or so it seems. One thing that lasts is the heavenly intercession on your behalf of Jesus Christ our great High Priest!

"Oh, come on, Sam. Don't exaggerate. Are you saying that Jesus continues to live to make intercession for me, even when I prove faithless and fickle, and keep failing in committing the same sins over and over and over again? Are you saying that nothing interrupts his presence at God's right hand on my behalf? What about the chaos in the Middle East? Doesn't he have to take a break interceding for me so he can attend to matters of far greater importance, like trying to arrange a cease-fire that will continue for more than twenty-four hours? Are you asking me to believe that when hurricanes and tornadoes and financial crises befall us that he doesn't at least take a fifteen-minute break to put things right?" That's right!

"Always? Really? Always? Forever? Are you sure it isn't only for as long as I prove worthy of his attention and love him perfectly and don't lose my temper with my spouse? Are you sure it isn't only for as long as I make him proud of me with my godly behavior?" Yes, I'm sure!

Try to envision what kind of Christian life we would lead if we genuinely and sincerely believed what these two words are saying! How might it affect the way you and I worship? Would any of us ever feel restrained in our shouts of joy? Would we ever grow weary of singing his praises? Would we ever again be embarrassed to kneel or raise our hands or clap or dance or weep or laugh? I don't think so.

If we grasped just a small measure of what these two words mean, there is simply no way to predict what our prayer lives would be like. We would never have to be encouraged to attend a prayer meeting. We would never struggle to volunteer in some capacity at our church. We would never have to be told to be generous and sacrificial in our giving to the financial needs of our local church. Never.

If you doubt what I'm saying, it must be that you still mistakenly think that "uttermost" means almost and that "always" means sometimes.

One final and critically important thing to note is the relationship between Christ's ability to save to the uttermost and the unending, incessant intercession he fulfills on our behalf. He is able to save to the uttermost those who draw near to God through him "since"—that is, "because," "for this reason," or "on these grounds"—he always lives to make intercession for them. Clearly, then, the fact that Jesus is always and forever on our side as he sits at the Father's right hand is the reason why we can have confidence that the salvation he gives us is complete and comprehensive and all-inclusive.

In other words, if Jesus did not always live to make intercession for us, he would not be able to save us. But "since" he "always" lives to represent us before the Father and to plead our case and to defend us against Satan's accusations, we can rest confidently in the salvation that he died and rose again to obtain. As the apostle John put it in 1 John 2:1, "We have an advocate with the Father, Jesus Christ the righteous."

That, then, is what God has done and is doing with our sin!

Conclusion

NOTWITHSTANDING ALL YOU'VE READ in the preceding pages, I'm sure some of you still have your doubts. In the interest of complete honesty, sometimes I do, too. I'm confident in what has been said about the many things God has done with my sin. I rejoice in knowing those things he will never do. But then, at some unusually stressful moment, the enemy sneaks in and sows the seeds of doubt. I can often hear myself saying, somewhere in the deep recesses of my soul, "But what if when you stand before God all the sins and failures and lapses in moral judgment come rushing back over you? Will they not swallow up all hope? Will they not destroy all joy?"

How are we to fight back against such insidious attacks? With what do we resist the enemy when he tries to undermine our confidence and hope in God? I can speak only for myself, but I immediately turn to the doxology that concludes the short epistle of Jude. My guess is that you know it well:

> Now to him who is able to keep you from stumbling and to present you blameless before the presence of his glory with great joy, to the only God, our Savior, through Jesus Christ our Lord, be glory, majesty, dominion, and authority, before all time and now and forever. Amen. (vv. 24–25)

My aim here isn't to unpack and explain this entire doxology, as worthy as it is of extensive discussion. Instead, I want to draw your attention to three phrases—or, better still, three words that I trust will supply you with the spiritual fuel to remain confident in your relationship with God. Perhaps the best way to approach the text is by asking three questions: What? Where? How?

First, look at *what* God is able to do for you. He is able—which is to say, utterly without limitation in his capacity as God—to present you "blameless" or without blemish. Being "without fault" or "blameless" or "without blemish" was the consistent requirement of God for all Old Testament sacrifices, indicating his requirement of absolute ethical perfection (see Ex. 29:1; Lev. 1:3; Num. 6:14; Ezek. 43:22); and such was the nature of Jesus Christ's sacrifice (see Heb. 9:14 and 1 Pet. 1:19).

Try to imagine what it will feel like to stand in God's glorious presence and feel no guilt, no shame, no fear, no embarrassment! For there will be nothing in you—whether physical or spiritual or psychological or emotional or sexual, not in your past, present, or future—to cause you to draw back or feel shame or hesitation. Nothing to disqualify you! Of course, the only reason this will be true is because of the many things we've seen that God has done with our sin.

If that weren't glorious enough, notice secondly *where* this will happen: "before the presence of his glory"! It's one thing to stand before other sinners and look at yourself in comparison with them. You might be able to envision that. But Jude is talking about standing boldly and confidently in the presence of the infinitely glorious God! Holy! Righteous in all his ways! Unfailing purity! His glory radiates and shines through and exposes all. Think about it. Your life will be presented before God's majesty, his glory, his goodness.

Does standing translucent before the blinding glory of God unsettle you? It shouldn't! And that is because of the dozen things God has done with your sin!

That's the what and the where, but look now at the *how*: "with great joy"! He doesn't say, "with great fear" or "apprehension" or "regret" or any such thing. The only affection that will flood your heart as you stand before the majesty and splendor of an infinitely holy God is joy! But joy in what or whom? Joy for what reason?

> It will be said on that day,
>> "Behold, this is our God; we have waited for him, that he
>> might save us.
>> This is the LORD; we have waited for him;
>> let us be glad and rejoice in his salvation." (Isa. 25:9)

> I will greatly rejoice in the LORD;
>> my soul shall exult in my God,
> for he has clothed me with the garments of salvation;
>> he has covered me with the robe of righteousness,
> as a bridegroom decks himself like a priest with a beautiful
>> headdress,
>> and as a bride adorns herself with her jewels. (61:10)

Such an experience will evoke pure, unadulterated joy! Sheer, unqualified, unsullied, unsoiled delight! Jubilation! This will also be a public celebration, a festival in God's presence of an innumerable multitude of forgiven saints, together praising, dancing, and singing to the glory of the God in whose presence they stand unafraid and accepted.

What is it that elicits such exuberant joy? Is it that we are blameless and without blemish, or is it that we are beholding the glory and splendor of God, forever in his presence? Without for a moment denying or diminishing the truth of the former, the answer is surely the latter.

If you were to poll professing Christians today, asking them, "What is the greatest gift of the gospel?" you would likely hear answers such as "forgiveness of sin," "adoption," "justification by faith," or any one of a number of wonderful blessings that come to us as a result of the work of Christ on the cross. I have no desire to belittle such blessings. They are glorious indeed. But their glory and greatness and blessedness are primarily in the degree to which they bring us to God. They are blessings only insofar as they make it possible for us to behold the beauty and splendor of God as revealed in the face of Jesus Christ.

What ultimately makes the gospel good news isn't that we get forgiven, saved, delivered, healed, renewed, justified, and adopted, as good and glorious as these experiences are. The gospel is good news because it gets us God! It overcomes every obstacle to our beholding the glory of God in the face of Jesus Christ for our everlasting enjoyment! As Piper says, "The saving love of God is God's commitment to do everything necessary to enthrall us with what is most deeply and durably satisfying, namely himself."[1] Furthermore, "If you could have heaven, with no sickness, and with all the friends you ever had on earth, and all the food you ever liked, and all the leisure activities you ever enjoyed, and all the natural beauties you ever saw, all the physical pleasures you ever tasted, and no human conflict or any

---

1   John Piper, *God Is the Gospel: Meditations on God's Love as the Gift of Himself* (Wheaton:, IL Crossway, 2005), 13.

natural disasters, could you be satisfied with heaven, if Christ was not there?"[2]

Gifts such as predestination, the incarnation of Christ, reconciliation, redemption in Christ's blood, even the consummation of our salvation at the second coming of Christ "are all good to the degree that they make possible the one great good—namely, knowing and enjoying God himself."[3] This, then, is the ground of our joy. This, then, is the reason we rejoice, because we get God in all his glory and majesty and dominion and authority. And we get God because of what he has done with our sin and what he has promised not to do with it.

2 Piper, *God Is the Gospel*, 15.
3 Piper, *God Is the Gospel*, 130.

General Index

Absalom, 72, 149–50
adoption, 20, 204
alien righteousness, 93
Alpha Centauri, 100
"always," 195–97
Ambrose of Milan, 43n10
Amnon, 149–50
Andromeda Galaxy, 100–101
Anselm, 43n10
anthropomorphism, 91, 145
assurance of salvation, 170
astronomy, 97–101
Athanasius, 43n10
atonement, models of, 36–37
Augustine, 43n10

Ballard, Robert, 124
Bancroft, C. L., 174–75
"because/therefore relationship with
    God," 181
"Before the Throne of God Above"
    (hymn), 174–75
beholding the beauty and splendor of
    God, 204–5
Bible, extravagant images and illustra-
    tions in, 103
Bible reading, 116
blameless, 202
blessed, 55, 61

blood of bulls and goats, 27, 28, 160
"blotting out," 131–33
Botox, 81
Bridges, Jerry, 126–27
Bunyan, John, 43n10

Calvin, John, 43n10
"carry away," 61
ceremonial purification, 73–74
child abuse, 39
Christian life, not "post" gospel, 179
Chrysostom, John, 43n10
clean heart, 74
cleansing from sin, 69–79
communion, 22
confession of sin, 23
conscience, 14–15
    defiled, 10, 14–15, 30, 57
    overly sensitive, 17
    purified, 25–27, 28
contextualization, 189
"cosmic child abuse," atonement as,
    38–39
cosmic transformation, 183
Covid-19 pandemic, 75–76
creation care, 190
curse, removal of, 183
cutting (self-harm), 30
Cyril of Alexandria, 43n10

Scripture Index

Also Available from Sam Storms

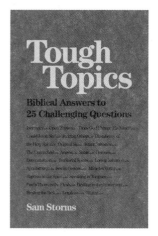

For more information, visit **crossway.org**.